The Cranfield New Entrepreneur

The Cranfield New Entrepreneur

Making Your Ideas Work

Peter Saunders

SIDGWICK & JACKSON
LONDON

First published in Great Britain in 1989
by Sidgwick & Jackson Limited
1 Tavistock Chambers, Bloomsbury Way
London WC1A 2SG

ISBN 0 283 99614 5

Photoset by Rowland Phototypesetting Limited
Bury St Edmunds, Suffolk
Printed in Great Britain by
Billing and Sons Limited, Worcester

To the women in my life:
Jackie, Catt, Tabby, Abigail and Miranda.

Contents

Acknowledgements

This book would not have been possible without all the people I have met on the programmes with which I have had involvement. I am extremely grateful for their input. I must express my thanks to Professors Paul Burns and Leo Murray, the first for placing me in a position to benefit and for his encouragement, and the second for agreeing to the use of Cranfield's name. In addition, I was pleased to receive permission to use materials from Dr Lyle Spencer of McBer and Co., and Colin Barrow of Cranfield.

Finally, I owe a large debt to Jenny Wheeley for sticking with the book and with me for so long.

Foreword

Everyone dreams of owning his or her own business. The dreams usually centre on giving the dreamer a better lifestyle: more money, status, autonomy, clothes, power or leisure. In these dreams the business could be anything: from becoming a jetsetting architect or a well respected adviser to owning a chain of toy shops or a restaurant.

People want to start businesses for all sorts of reasons. Many would like the opportunity of making more money – or at least having the chance to do so. Others want the freedom and autonomy that owning a business brings. There is the challenge of getting a successful venture off the ground. There is also a lot of excitement and fun.

The difficulty for most of us when trying to turn the dreams into reality is that we simply have no idea of what business to start – we all complain that it is hard to spot business ideas, but in reality, they exist in their hundreds and thousands in the environment around us. It is simply that we persist in our refusal to recognize them.

The examples used in this book are real businesses, with details changed where necessary. Statements made about firms are my own opinions and interpretations of circumstances and may differ from the interpretations placed on the circumstances by the individuals involved.

PART I: GUIDING YOUR SEARCH

It is pointless generating business ideas, launching the idea and then, for some reason or another, finding that the business does not suit *you*. There are many factors, unique to you and to your environment, which will influence the definition of what is a 'suitable' idea in your mind. The chapters in this section are intended to give you a framework into which you can fit the ideas you generate to ascertain if they are suitable for you.

Because owning and running a business is not easy, you will have to remember and be able to deal with the following factors:

- there is high risk in starting a business and it is not just a job
- there will be financial hardship in the early years
- there is high stress associated with owning a business
- it involves long hours
- there will be damage to your family and social life
- it will often be lonely

You will have to ask yourself the following questions:

- will I enjoy it?
- how much time am I willing to devote to it?
- what am I good at?
- how much money have I got?
- is there a market?

Getting stuck in a business for which you have lost motivation can be heartrending for you and those around you. Using the guidelines laid out in this section will help you to understand what sort of business best achieves your goals, is within your resources, and fits your own personal talents.

Chapter One:
Personal Objectives and Constraints

Introduction

It has been said that any road will do for the person who does not know where he is going. This is as true of business as it is anything else. A business's objectives such as market share or profitability are simply derived from the objectives of the individual who owns and runs it. When the firm is large and the directors and managers do not own it, the objectives are an amalgamation of the personal objectives of the various 'stakeholders' in the company. Stakeholders in this sense include quite a large variety of people – the directors, shareholders, employees, customers, lenders, government, etc. Each of these will affect the company's objectives and how they are set, but they will not all have the same degree of power over the process.

When looking at new businesses, the influence of personal objectives is all persuading. A business that is closely controlled and operated by one person will be an extension of that person's personality. For example:

> If your objectives lean towards achieving more leisure time and more social life, then it is a waste of energy even considering an idea which will involve you selling through a high street retail outlet. In that type of business you work 7 a.m. to 11 p.m., six (or even seven) days a week. You will be far too tired to enjoy the social life, even if you have time to find it.

> Ian, a successful production manager for a manufacturer of electronic products, felt that he was not getting on quickly enough in career terms. He wanted to be managing director but thought it an unlikely achievement in his current firm.

> He set up a firm of his own simply to become managing director. He enjoyed being the managing director of a very small firm far more than being the boss (as he was) of more than a hundred people in his previous firm. Things ran smoothly until the commercial realities set in: his initial capital ran out and he did not have enough sales to support himself.

If you do not know what your objectives are, you will have no way of measuring your success. People often regard 'success' as, for instance, owning a Rolls Royce, or some other trapping of wealth. This can only be considered success if that individual's objectives include both wealth and the desire to flaunt it: a Rolls Royce's major attribute is not that it is a car but that it says of its owner 'look at me I'm wealthy'.

There is no single definition of success; it can only be measured in personal terms. Suppose your major objective is the desire to control your own destiny – a desire not to work for anyone else, known in my trade as the drive for 'autonomy'. You can achieve it very easily by giving up work and relying on the State provision, such as it is. Even if you combine your desire for autonomy with a desire to be independent of State support, you could still achieve it by setting up a business which, at best, would never provide more than a living wage. This could therefore be described as a success. By other people's objectives this is failure. In other words, you have to use your own goals as a measuring stick against which to compare your subsequent performance. You must first create the measuring stick: setting objectives for where you want to be thus enabling you to judge whether or not you are successful.

As a result, it is important for you to examine your own personal objectives before selecting a business idea. At the very least it will help you evaluate the ideas you generate and it could directly help in the generation of the ideas themselves.

> Ray Jones decided that he'd had enough of helping other people to make money and decided to 'go it alone'. He really wanted to use the contacts he'd built up over a number of years as a concierge in the hotels he had worked for. He had also enjoyed setting up for guests tours or nights out at the theatre and therefore combined the two by setting up a company in corporate entertaining.

I speak of 'examining one's objectives', which is easy enough for those of us who already know where they are going. Many people do not make their objectives so explicit: they often confine themselves to knowing what makes them either happy or unhappy in life, and leave it at that. This approach is fine normally, but simply disastrous in a business where so much is at risk and one usually only gets one chance. It's important to get it right first time. It is not really necessary to know beforehand whether you will enjoy going to see, say, a new play because you lose very little if you do not get the expected enjoyment. It is an entirely different matter to find after six months that the business you have sunk your life savings into is making you very unhappy – even if it might be performing very well.

> Belinda McDougal had wanted to set up her own business for a long time. She wanted to be able to influence her own future. She decided to set up a restaurant and started looking round for premises, while at the same time, gaining experience by working as a waitress in a competing chain of restaurants. After a long, hard struggle she found the ideal premises and opened her doors for trade. At the end of a reasonably successful first six months, her boyfriend of long standing had left her and she was very close to a nervous breakdown. Through these personal difficulties and the pressures of hard work, Belinda had also lost motivation and this was causing the trade she had so assiduously built up to slide. Essentially her self-confessed problem was that she had simply not taken into account her strong need for a social life which did not revolve around her work. Most of all, she missed not being able to get to the theatre.

If you are currently in the position of not having explicit objectives, you need to set some that you will be satisfied and happy with.

In addition to understanding your objectives, it is also worth taking into account the constraints that inhibit your choice of business. Most of us suffer from a common constraint: we do not have a great deal of money to throw into a business and are therefore restricted in some way from starting up just any business.

Personal Objectives

Types of objectives

There are three types of objectives which need to be considered: long, medium and short term.

Long term

Long term objectives could be considered 'life goals': things which you would be happy achieving during your life. The time horizon involved is usually considered to be in excess of five years. They are the most important to you as they are the ones which determine all other goals.

> One of the long term goals of Ray Roberts, an employee at Rothmans, is to be in such a position that when he retires, he need never have to worry about money again. For him this means an income, in today's terms, of £100,000 per annum from the age of sixty for the rest of his life.

Medium term

Medium term objectives are derived from long term objectives and are definable large achievements of part of the longer term goals. You would usually set up these objectives with a time horizon of more than one year but less than ten, or more commonly, five.

> There are a number of ways that Ray could achieve his retirement income objective. The suggestions must number in their hundreds, but here are three:
>
> - become a senior partner in a major accounting firm
> - become a main board director of his employer (Rothmans)
> - start and sell his own successful business.
>
> To achieve the first suggestion, a medium term goal that Ray would have to achieve would be to qualify as an accountant. To achieve the second, his medium term goal might be to become a director of the subsidiary he currently works for. For success in the third, he must have a medium term goal of owning and operating a reasonably successful business.

Short term

Short term objectives are those steps along the road to achieving medium term goals. They usually take up to a year to attain.

For Ray's first medium term objective, he should have the following short term goals:

- getting a job with a major firm of accountants
- signing a training contract
- finding a study course to help him pass the first set of exams.

For his second objective, Ray might have these short term goals:

- finding a new brand worthy of commercialization
- setting up launch plans
- putting the plans into operation

For Ray's third medium term objective, he might:

- find an idea he would be happy with which has commercial opportunities
- research the idea
- get finance
- obtain premises
- resign from Rothmans
- launch his business

With regard to Ray, I deliberately failed to tell you that another of his long term objectives is to achieve control of his own destiny so consequently the first and second alternatives were not ideally open to him. He founded a specialized market research company.

'Step down' objectives

As you can see from the Ray Roberts example, goals are all interconnected and all stem from the long term goals. Hence the importance of these – they control what you should set as both medium *and* short term goals.

Take Ray's long term objective: that of achieving a comfortable retirement income. It and its associated goals can be written down as follows:

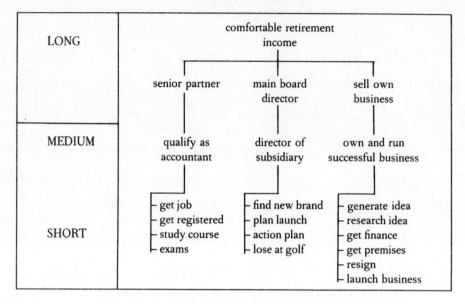

Having first set your objectives, it would be beneficial to draw a similar diagram for yourself: it helps you think more clearly about what you want to achieve.

Areas susceptible to goal setting

If you have ever set yourself any explicit objectives, you have probably confined them to business and career goals. Why restrict yourself in this way if you believe, as I do, that this goal-setting process is vital to achieving anything easily or effectively?

I believe that it is important to set objectives in all areas of life. The categories I use are:

> *Family*
>> – Anyone can be a father but few can be a 'dad' to their children.
>> – I would like an enjoyable relationship with my wife.
>
> *Lifestyle*
>> – I would like a sailing boat and the opportunity to use it.
>> – I would like a gofer-chauffeur (try saying that to yourself a few times!)
>
> *Health*
>> – I am a 'fat forty' and would like to be a 'fit forty'.

Career/Business
- I would like to have the chair (professorship) of enterprise at a major university.
- I would like my entrepreneurial earnings to be triple their current level.

Note also: my personal objectives are determining my business goals. Since I want lifestyle improvements combined with a chair careerwise, I must triple my outside earnings (university staff, even professors, are not the most highly paid people).

Incidentally, the list is not complete because objectives are very personal. All of them were derived from a long term objective: I want to achieve peace of mind. These are some of the things that will help *me* to achieve that. Note that the definition of 'peace of mind' is personal to me and involves money; someone else might also have the objective of 'peace of mind' but will achieve it by taking vows and joining a silent order of monks.

How do you set objectives?

Given that most of us rarely make our personal goals explicit, it is not surprising that few of us have looked at the goal setting process. We tend, perhaps, to see other people's positions, environments, families, businesses, careers, etc., and say to ourselves 'I would quite like that'. Or perhaps we see a car, boat, house or another material possession and want that too. What we often fail to do is to examine ourselves to see what it is that makes us happy and fulfilled in life.

It is by asking yourself questions like: what do I enjoy? what do I do well? what motivates me? that you will be able to develop explicit goals, rather than wallow in ill-formed and vague desires. When you try to do it, use a pen and paper – there is nothing like writing down objectives to help clarify them. Because they are in black and white, you tend to examine them more closely for accuracy. To refine them, do the examination two, three or as many times as is necessary to develop a list that you are happy with.

What do you enjoy?

Many people find it hard to admit what they enjoy; preferring to define it as the reverse of what they do not enjoy. Negative approachs are rarely satisfying because simply eliminating what you do not enjoy leaves you with not only the things that are enjoyed, but also those that you are indifferent to. As motivation will be one of the major determinants of subsequent success, it is preferable to be doing something that you actively *like* doing.

Robert Nathan, a director of Career Counselling Services, has developed a technique for allowing you to examine yourself in this area through the use of self-inspection of values and interests.

Values

What values do you place on your activities? There are many different reasons why you might perform a particular activity. For example, you undoubtedly help others from time to time, but do you like doing this most of the time? You certainly will have times when you prefer to be on your own, but do you want *this* most of the time? Examine the following list of values, giving each a rating in terms of how important it is to you.

Social: being respected by other people, belonging to a group, having an active family life, being strong in religious practice.

Altruistic: being charitable, enjoying helping others with or without reward.

Economic: making lots of money.

Achievement: accomplishing difficult things, taking risks, having responsibility, using skill and judgement, having competition.

Power: being well known, leading others, influencing others, being a recognized expert.

Learning: seeking knowledge, learning new skills.

Variety: changing people, activities, surroundings.

Independence: having discretion in decisions, working alone, working at one's own pace.

Creativity: developing new ideas, devices and artistic creations.

Lifestyle: living simply, living the high life, being busy, being free.

Now write them down in the order of their importance to you and go on to do the same for your interests.

Interests

This area has some overlap with the values above. You should look at the following list and again give a rating of how important each of them is to you. Are you interested in activities which are:

- practical: having a definite end product

- outdoor
- investigative: where ideas and analysis dominate
- artistic
- creative
- social
- give you the feeling that you have helped others: teaching
- enterprising
- involve leading others: selling
- conventional

Again, write them down in the order of their importance to you.

Your work

What is it you enjoy about your current work? Your past jobs? Is it the:

- opportunity – to use your skills, do what you are interested in, satisfy your values, develop your capabilities, mix with like-minded people?
- ability – to solve technical and professional problems, to use your time effectively, to get on with your peers, subordinates and bosses?
- status – salary, car, secretary, other perks?

Write them down in the order of importance to you.

What do you do well?

Here too, Robert Nathan's analysis can help. He suggests that you divide a page into two and on the left hand side write a list of anything you have done which pleased you in some way – preferably something that left you with a sense of achievement, pride or fulfilment. On the right hand side list all the skills, knowledge and experience that were needed to perform the activity and also those which resulted from it.

Skills

- ideas and information
- analysing, budgeting, checking, classifying
- initiating, memorizing
- things/products
- co-ordinating, operating, producing
- people

–   advising, counselling, listening, managing, persuading, serving, taking instructions, teaching.

Knowledge

Did you need some knowledge to be able to apply the skills you used? What was it?

Experience

Experience in certain tasks gives us skills and knowledge and could help us develop attitudes.

What motivates you?

After you have prepared the list of positive things that you have done go through it a second time. This time write down what it was that caused you to start the activity. Was it:

–   the chance to pursue an idea?
–   the desire for social rewards?
–   profit-oriented?
–   job dissatisfaction related?

After all of this you should be awash with lists of all sorts. Examine them to see what the top five to ten recurring themes are. This top ten are your most important interests, values, motivation, and abilities, and you can now use them to help yourself in the development of personal goals. Write down the goals as you develop them in your mind.

If you still feel uncomfortable with the goals you have developed, go back through the lists to re-examine the priorities that you gave each factor. Do not be afraid to repeat these exercises, from scratch if necessary, until you have a list of goals that you are happy with.

Day-dreaming

Another way of helping to determine what your long term objectives are is to establish 'lifetime' goals though a form of guided day-dreaming. Day-dreams and visions can be very useful thing in helping you to come to an understanding of what you want out of life. You can best achieve a guided day-dream by:

- finding somewhere quiet for a while
- sitting down, with pen and paper
- imagining yourself to be at the closing days of your life
- dreaming that it has been a happy and fruitful time: you have had a marvellous life for which you are very grateful.
- expanding the vision so as to be able to see what it is that has made it happy and fruitful – what did you achieve that makes you so happy?
- writing down the achievements. Try these on, like hats, to see if you can use them as long term objectives.

These achievements could be what will make you happy in the long term: you will have established some lifetime goals.

The objective/strategy questions

What appear to be objectives in my earlier list are pretty well useless in their current form: what does being a 'dad' to ones children mean? It is as bad as the concept 'I want to be happy'. To make them useful you have to make them more concrete by turning them into strategy goals. You can do this by asking yourself certain questions. A desire for anything at all remains a dream rather than an objective (or strategy goal) until you can clearly answer three questions about it.

- where am I going?
- when will I get there?
- how will I know that I have arrived?

Where am I going?

This is the statement of the basic goal: 'I want to achieve ...' It may be something that is relatively simple in interpretation, for instance, the winning of my professorship. However, it could also be something far more complex and nebulous like my own personal 'dad to my children' dream. To turn such a dream into a basic statement of what you want to do, you have to be capable of defining more clearly just what it means to you. For example, my interpretation of this objective might involve spending more time with the kids, teaching them to read, allowing them their own independence, gaining their trust and love. For every objective, it is necessary to define what each factor means to you personally.

When will I get there?

Having a basic statement of where you want to get to is useless on its own – you must set a date for its achievement. In the case of the professorship, I have set myself a goal of ten years from the time of writing.

How will I know that I have arrived?

Again, in addition to a basic statement of where you want to go and an associated time horizon, you need a method of knowing that you have arrived. You need to quantify it in some way. I will know I have arrived when a major university appoints me to a chair. Or will I? What does 'major' mean? Having asked the question of yourself, you will now be able to see more clearly which are long term and which are short. For me the chair is a long-term objective and the tripling of my business earnings is short to medium term.

In addition, you will now be in a position to ask yourself 'how do I go about achieving these objectives?' In other words, what strategies will help me to achieve my goals.

Written in stone?

Once you have got some acceptable explicit goals, should they be written in stone and hence unchanging? At this point in time, you probably will have only just started the goal-setting process. Goals need refining. Do the exercises several times over, preferably when you are in different moods. Try visions on for size – do they fit you? Would you truly be happy with that? Would you be able to look back at the end of your life and say: 'it was worth it'?

Try to avoid goals that either too easy or too difficult to achieve; easily achieved goals are both less rewarding, and require less motivation – inevitably linked with career lethargy. Moreover, when an objective doesn't require your best efforts, you won't give them. If your goals are too hard it becomes increasingly difficult to have confidence in yourself and giving up becomes a viable alternative. Even after you have arrived at a set of goals you feel happy to work towards, you still should not feel constrained to keeping them static. As you start achieving the earlier ones and gain more experience on your chosen path, your perceptions of the attractiveness of the longer term ones will almost certainly change and in many cases expand.

As a counsellor to hundreds of new ventures, I advise that each company not only plan in detail for the launch and the early operations, but that they continue to plan their own (business) destinies, re-evaluating their plans for the next year, each year. This planning process by its very nature causes the business to re-evaluate its business objectives, which in turn causes a re-evaluation of personal objectives.

Goals are *not* written in stone and change over time.

Constraints

The world would be a far different place if we could simply create goals for ourselves and then simply set out to achieve them. The reality is that we are constrained from doing exactly as we please in very many areas of our lives by all sorts of factors. These factors tend to fall into three major categories: other people (our stakeholders); our resources (or more often our lack of resources); and our lack of knowledge, experience and skills.

Other people/stakeholders

When a large company sets its objectives it should take into account that there are people and organizations outside it, but with an interest in it, who ought to be taken into account. These are known either as stakeholders (if they demand a share in the wealth created by the firm) or as pressure groups (if they want recognition and managerial response). For a company, stakeholders and pressure groups might include the:

- shareholders
- suppliers
- competitors
- unions
- employees
- government
- public
- customers
- financial institutions
- media

All will have some influence over the outcome of the goal setting process. When setting goals on a personal level we too have to remember that there are stakeholders and pressure groups in our lives. Who are your stakeholders – the people who want a share of the wealth and environments you create? The most obvious is your spouse and your children. How do these constrain your actions and choices? There are four major areas: income, time, family matters, and support.

Income

If your spouse does not work and therefore cannot financially support the family during the early, lean periods of a business then you have to either choose a business which is going to be capable of supporting you all from a very early stage or get that much more from your financial backers to cover this period.

> Andy Mallinson has set up a company called Odessy. His first sales were only expected six months after launch, and even then would be relatively slow in growing. He needed to borrow just to live for the first year.

Time

Again, if you do have a spouse and/or children, you will quite naturally want to spend some time with them. This means choosing a business idea which will allow you some free time. Further, it's important to remember that there are only 24 hours in a day. Expect to sleep some of them.

Family matters

If your spouse has a career, how will your choice of business affect that? A solicitor is not going to regard a shady scrap metal dealer as an ideal life partner! Do you want to create a dynasty (and I do not mean produce or direct the TV programme)? If so, you will have to choose a business which is capable of employing family members and has longevity.

> Roy Limb set up a firm installing air conditioning systems. Since the pension he was being paid at the time of launch exceeded most peoples' salaries, he was not doing it for money. In fact, one of his stated objectives was to create something that he could pass on to his sons.

The above are only two examples of 'family matters'. I am sure that a dozen others spring to mind, but if not, I am sure they will if you ask yourself 'what do the members of my family want of any business I might set up?' Even better, ask them instead!

Support and motivation

Starting your own business creates tremendously large pressures on you. You will definitely need some moral support from somewhere, preferably your family. You will need motivating when your spirits are low, as they undoubtedly can be. Will your family help here? If not, you are going to need to set up a business which minimizes the strain on you.

> One man, who will remain nameless, came to Cranfield for help in setting up what appeared to be an attractive business. A few days after being offered a place on one of our programmes, he rang to say he would not take up the offer since his wife had said 'it is the business or me'! He was probably wise not to start.

Resources

Our lack of resources constrain us in many ways. There are three categories of resources available to most people: money, people, and materials.

Money

Virtually all businesses need some money to start them off. Some need very little; the classic example is window cleaning. Others need quite a lot; for instance, a nuclear-powered electricity generating station. The type of business you choose will determine how much money you need and, if you do not have sufficient funds, you will have to make a different choice.

> Norman Pogson started his business with very little money. He simply put together a catalogue of kitchen equipment from suppliers he was reasonably sure of and then hit the road to sell to kitchen equipment retailers.

You can borrow to increase the amount available, it is true, but traditional bank lending is on a one to one basis: if you have £10,000, they will put up £10,000. So, if you have only £1,000 then you need to start a business which needs only £2,000. It does not work out quite like that in practice because at the smaller end, bank managers are often willing to 'take a view', that is to lend outside the traditional norms. There is the government's 'Loan Guarantee

Scheme' which also throws the relationships out of kilter. Actually, money is not the biggest constraint – as people often believe. Money will always be found in some way for a good, well-presented idea. There are all sorts of routes to raising money where necessary.

People

In the early days of a business the resources available to hire labour are very scarce. What labour is available to you, either full time or part time? Remember that your family can only be depended on for so long.

Materials

Do you have any physical resources that can be put to good use in the business? If not, and if they are necessary, you will have to buy them. Are you restricted to using your own home for some reason? All of these factors are constraints.

Knowledge/experience/skills

The number of things that are outside your experience and skills is probably infinitely large. Consequently, it is certainly possible that the business you choose will need skills you do not possess. The absence of experience does not make starting that business impossible – just that much harder.

> David Bruce, the founder of Bruce's Breweries, also known as the 'Firkin' pubs (recently put up for sale at £6 million), had so little skill when he started that he did not even know what prices to charge. He took a look at a pub down the road and added five pence to everything.

It is far better to start a business that is within the scope of your knowledge, experience and skills because you will almost certainly do it more professionally. However, you could always buy the skills in, if you have the money.

Achieving objectives

Right – so now you have a set of specific, explicit goals. What do you do with them? How do you achieve them? It is very simple. To achieve *long-term goals*, you must first achieve the various *medium-term goals* which compose them. To achieve medium term goals, you must first achieve the various *short-term goals* of which they are comprised.

Thus, to achieve all goals means first achieving your short-term goals. Let me digress a little before going on to describe the routes to success.

Using time

Do you use a 'to do' list: things you have to do today? If you do, go and find it. If you do not, spend a few moments compiling one – what are the most pressing tasks to be done today or tomorrow? Write them down. Take the list and compare it with another of the many lists you will have written out by now: the list of short-term objectives. If you are a fairly normal person, there will be a number of tasks on your 'to do' list which do not go towards achieving any of your short-term goals. There are two reasons why these discrepancies could arise, both of which are very important to you and to your objectives:

Your short term goal list is incomplete – meaning that the exercises you went through to compile it did not cover the whole ground.
You are getting side-tracked into doing tasks which do not achieve any of your short-term goals – you are wasting very valuable time.

There should not be any discrepancy whatsoever if you are using your time effectively. If you use a 'to do' list which is based on achieving your short term goals, you will use your time far more effectively.

Activities and tasks

One way of developing a list of things to do which all go towards achieving your short-term objectives, and hence getting towards your goals, is to break down your short-term goals into 'activities' or 'tasks'. In this sense an activity or task is one more step along the road to achieving the objective.

Suppose that a short term-goal on your list is to generate ideas for a business venture that you want to launch (as part of your medium- and long-term goals). First you need to look at what steps you might have to undertake to achieve that goal. For the idea generation goal they might be, as a starting point:

–   finish reading this book
–   set up brainstorming session
–   develop some morphological analyses (see later)
–   see the local enterprise agency

- scan the business opportunity publications
- apply an initial filter to the ideas to see if they fit *you*

You now have a series of activities which all go towards achieving that goal. If you break the activities down into tasks, each taking no longer than two or three hours, you can put them into your diary so that they now become specific tasks for particular days. Provided that you actually do the tasks you set for yourself in this way, then you have a system which allows you to start achieving short-term goals. And of course achieving short-term goals achieves medium-term goals, and of course achieving them. . . .

Out of sight

Writing down your objectives and keeping them close to you means that they will not be out of sight and hence out of mind:

> George Pearson made the achievement of £1 million in personal wealth by the age of thirty his major goal. He always kept this goal in his pocket written down so that each time he put his hand in his pocket he would be reminded of it. I asked him (when he was thirty-two) whether or not he had achieved it, and in reply he simply took a piece of paper from his pocket. It read '£5,000,000 by age 35'.

Conclusion

Businesses which perform well usually have a good strategy regarding such things as marketing, production and finance. In fact, it is often said that a good strategy is essential if a business is to be successful. In this sense, and at its simplest, a strategy is just a statement of how you plan to get your business where you want it to go, and a strategy can only be good or bad in terms of whether it will get the business to where you want it to be. Thus a business cannot develop a 'good' strategy until you know where you want it to go. A business must have targets, goals and objectives.

In your case, in common with all other people who run their own businesses, the business targets and goals will be derived from what you personally want to achieve. This means that long before you can launch a business you have to know what your personal objectives are so that you can:

- evaluate the business ideas that you generate from using this book – ideas themselves can only be good or bad from the viewpoint of your objectives, and
- develop business objectives which will subsequently allow valid strategies to be developed.

Finally, when developing objectives, you must keep in mind that you are constrained from doing absolutely anything you want by both the people around you who have a stake in what you do, and by the extent of the resources available to you.

Chapter Two:
Qualities for Success

Introduction

It is extremely difficult to distinguish a 'good' entrepreneur from a 'bad' entrepreneur. Some similarities between good entrepreneurs do exist and this knowledge can be of help to anyone who proposes to start a business. Are you an extroverted or introverted person? Are you self-confident or self-conscious? The answers to such questions can be very important to you when developing ideas for future businesses. Take extroversion:

- extroversion can be seen as a very desirable character trait to possess if you are planning to start a business which involves, say, door-to-door selling
- extroversion can be seen as a very undesirable character trait to possess if you are planning to start a business which involves something like funeral parlours.

Any character trait can be seen either as a strength or as a weakness depending on the context of the business to be started. If you can identify your own traits you can use them in helping yourself both in the generation of ideas and their subsequent evaluation.

It is generally believed that there are several character traits which will help towards becoming successful in a new business. If this is true, and the available research does seem to back this proposition up to some extent, then a person who is weak in some of the areas that the chosen business dictates are essential, must find alternatives to strengthen his or her position or adopt one which requires less of those particular traits. As a result, you must take a long and hard look at both the character traits which seem most common in 'successful' entrepreneurs, and at yourself.

Common 'Success' Character Traits

There are many different character traits and qualities that you should have as a burgeoning entrepreneur in an ideal world. This section shows the most important many of which boil down to the following:

- your motivation
- your versatility
- your professionalism
- how business-orientated you are
- your possession of certain 'required' character traits
- how healthy you are.

Your motivation

The strength of your commitment to an idea is increasingly being seen as the most important factor in your psychological make-up as a new business person. Having dedication, drive and being totally committed to your idea will almost certainly help it to succeed. It would probably be better to turn that round – unless you have dedication, drive and are totally committed to the prospective business – I guarantee you failure.

Sadly, I cannot say that the presence of this factor guarantees success: if it were that simple, all you would have to do is motivate yourself towards an idea, and it would become an instantaneous success. However, if you do not have this motivation you are likely to fold at the first major hurdle that crosses your path, and that would be a waste of time for all concerned.

> Elona Bryant was a museum curator for a local authority. The authority decided to close the museum to save money and Elona lost her job. She had some quite specialized knowledge of a particular field and thought that she would open a shop dealing in antiques. She began buying at auctions and collected a reasonably sized stock. Then she started looking round for premises and found that the people she would be selling to were partial to Bond Street shopping. She perceived, correctly or not, that if she did not get a Bond Street location, the business would not succeed. She decided that getting such a shop was beyond her, and as a result she decided not to go into business, getting a job instead, outside her field and interests, and sold the stock (again through auction houses).

Versatility

When anyone starts a business they usually have to operate with restrictions of some kind – often lack of money – and this means that the owner/founder will have to be a very versatile and well-rounded person: he or she will not always be able to hire all the various people who may be necessary to the success of the business. Any business needs a marketing person along with someone who will handle the production of the goods or services, because the provision and selling of goods and services is what business is all about. It needs someone who understands finance and accountancy, to keep score. Where the business employs anyone other than the owner, someone has to perform a personnel function. Where a business has a toilet – it has to have a cleaner. When you start a business all these different capacities are yours.

Can you handle all the various tasks that your business will set for you? You will forever be trying to do a number of things at once: type the invoices for yesterday's deliveries, while trying to package the deliveries ready for tomorrow along with attempting to finish last week's bookkeeping. And you'll find you're doing it all on a Sunday evening at 11.30 pm. You *must* be willing to get your hands dirty.

> John Douglas, the founder and managing director of Penforth Sofa-Beds Ltd, still spends as many days on the factory floor as his selling activities will allow, even though he now has twenty people working for him. And I do mean factory floor – he tidies (essential in a factory) and cleans: he even cleans the toilet. His employees do not think of him as meddling because most of them are on piecework: where they are only paid for what is produced. What he does not do they'd have to do for themselves and lose valuable time (or not have a particularly pleasant work environment).

Professionalism

Professionalism is vital to the success of most ideas: your customers, whether corporate or individual, value a working and well-presented product or service. Being professional means paying a lot of attention to detail and being meticulous in ensuring that the service or the goods themselves are up to the quality that the customer expects. Being unprofessional naturally knocks your credibility as a supplier. Concentrating on the small things can bring very large dividends:

> Recently I participated in a social event organized by the managing director, Ray Jones, of a business founded only four months ago to provide corporate entertainment. Let me run through the evening for you. At 5 pm we were picked up by a somewhat luxurious

coach for the trip to London. It had tables, TVs, toilets, and most importantly, a large bar. Admittedly, it was a second hand coach, but the previous owner (a member of the Royal Family who used it for transporting a polo team around) had left it in pretty reasonable condition. The hour and a half it took to get to London passed by unnoticed. We then went to the Mountbatten Hotel for a buffet dinner (and drinks), and on to a West-end show called 'Run for your Wife'. The coach then took us back to our hotel.

The professionalism involved was demonstrated (and appreciated) in a number of ways:

- the client (me, in this case) had nothing more difficult to do than remember whether to turn right out of the theatre or left to get to the coach, which was not particularly hard since it was parked in full view less than fifty yards away. The client was able to enjoy him or herself completely without distraction. I even saw the organizers doing the appropriate tipping.
- they got the (pre-ordered) interval drink requirements exactly right, even down to the ice and lemon, for thirty people
- at some point between dropping us off at the Mountbatten and picking us up after the theatre, the bar on the coach had been completely restocked for the return journey, which passed even more unnoticed than the outward leg.

It was altogether a very enjoyable evening.

Business orientation

If you are going to be a success at business you need to be business minded. Many people start businesses which are not intended to make lots of money, and this is fine, but don't forget that we are talking about *your* money here.

Your new business may be your only source of income and must therefore achieve at least a living wage for you.

Whether you are planning to go into business for profits or for fun (and the two are not mutually exclusive as has been proved to my satisfaction) you must be results-orientated. This means setting yourself objectives and trying to attain them, otherwise you simply have no idea what you are trying to attain.

You must have focus. To be professional, you should concentrate on doing well whatever it is that the business entails, avoiding the sidetracks that often come to take your attention away from the mainstream of your business.

Penforth Sofa-Beds used to have its own transport. It used to manufacture the wooden frames itself. John now subcontracts the delivery and buys in already manufactured frames and this allows Penforth to concentrate more effectively on what it does well: the marketing of sofa-beds.

You must be innovative, different in some way or why should customers change from their existing source of supply and buy from you?

Finally, you need to be a professional risk-taker. Anyone can take risks, especially with money – just look in any bookie's outlet. The 'professional' risk-taker, in business terms, is one who matches the level of risk inherent in any proposition with the potential rewards, money or otherwise. If it is going to be more than normally risky, a professional risk-taker will want more than normal returns.

Required traits

There are many traits it would be advisable to possess if you are to be successful in business. One study[1] suggests that the entrepreneurship level is high if the owner is:

- informal
- driven by opportunity
- tolerant of ambiguity
- persistent/persevering
- enthusiastic
- dynamic
- good at networking
- good at communicating
- highly independent
- achievement oriented

If you are a woman, it has been suggested that you need the following factors in addition to those needed by female managers in larger businesses[2]:

- low conformity
- high energy level
- lower interpersonal skills

1 Stuart R., and Abettit P. A., 'Field Study of Start-up Ventures – Part II: Predicting Initial Success', Frontiers of Entrepreneurship Research, 1986, Babson College, Mass., USA.
2 Sexton D. L. and Bowman N. B., 'Validation of a Personality Index: Comparative Psychological Characteristics Analysis of Female Entrepreneurs, Managers, Entrepreneurship Students and Business Students', Frontiers of Entrepreneurship Research, 1986, Babson College, Mass., USA.

- higher risk-taking abilities
- higher social adroitness
- high autonomy
- tolerance for change
- harm avoidance
- less interested in succour

If you are Irish, we can describe exactly what qualities it is suggested you would have, all the way down to your parental relationships! According to another study[1] Irish entrepreneurs are:

- male: circa 40 years old
- first born in a middle class family
- close to their mothers
- like their father in personality
- married with three children
- earning c £20,000 in 1984
- married to a wife earning c £15,000
- from Dublin, Limerick or Cork
- of uneducated parents (but middle class nonetheless! – see the second finding)
- managerially experienced
- independent
- energetic
- goal-oriented
- competitive
- flexible
- good with people

Another study[2] showed that women were generally more effective than men in the management of their businesses – which some would say is only right.

It can therefore be seen that there are a number of common themes running through all of these studies. You should be:

- resilient
- self-confident
- wanting the challenge
- ruthless
- having an internal locus of control
- deprived emotionally, financially, intellectually or in some other way.

1 Hisrich R. D., O'Cinneide B., 'The Irish Entrepreneur: Characteristics, Problems, And Future Success', Frontiers of Entrepreneurship Research, 1986, Babson College, Mass., USA.
2 Birley S., Moss C. and Saunders P., 'The Differences Between Small Firms Started By Male And Female Entrepreneurs Who Attended Small Business Courses', Frontiers of Entrepreneurship Research, 1986, Babson College, Mass., USA.

Resilience

The most common word heard by the new business person is 'no'. You have to be able to bounce back from a large number of set-backs and refusals.

> Steven Carpenter wanted to set up a business retailing cut price jewellery in South East London. He approached six different Bank managers before getting a positive response.

Self-confidence

A lack of self-confidence will come across clearly to anyone you are dealing with. It can be a major disadvantage in selling because your customers will regard it as a disbelief in your own products or services. Confidence in oneself is also a source of motivation and, of course, pride. These qualities are essential to success.

Wanting a challenge

This is the most common reason why people start businesses (it isn't always money!). Starting a business is a big challenge, so it is an asset if that you find excitement motivating.

Ruthless

It is your pocket that will be affected by the success or failure of your venture. If you do not quickly develop ruthlessness (that is, if you do not already have it) you will find yourself doing all sorts of things which are not in your best interest. Ruthlessness requires courage and can develop self-confidence.

Internal locus of control

All this means is that the entrepreneur must care more about achieving targets that he or she has set for him/herself than for targets that have been set by his or her external environment. The trappings of success are less important than the success itself.

Deprived

A colleague of mine (Professor Malcolm Harper) has developed a theory regarding why people start businesses which I call the 'Cataclysmic Approach to New Business Formation'. He has looked at the process of small business formation around the world and has come up with the opinion that people only start businesses when they have had some sort of jolt – making them dissatisfied with their current lot in life. Malcolm cites many examples, including the Jews, who have been jolted from pillar to post for the last 2,000 years, the Ugandan Asians, the Germans and Japanese. He includes the last two because they lost wars: leading to the conclusion that atomic war must be good for a country's inspiration (thus my name for his theory). It is certainly possible, and research does seem to prove, that members of minority groups do well in business. On a personal level, you might experience a similar jolt from, say, being moved by your employer to a new job or part of the country you do not enjoy. The classic employee's jolt is redundancy, but it could equally come from a major change in your own aspirations.

Health

You are going to find that starting and running a business takes energy, both physical and mental. Consequently, you need to be physically and mentally healthy.

> Finally, if you do not fit into any of these categories you need not worry too much, since (yet) another study[1] has shown that there is little relationship between psychological attributes and subsequent financial performance.

Assessing yourself

Ideally, it would be best to have someone else assess your character traits because they would certainly be more objective and hence the results more reliable. However, that route is not always easy and consequently we have to rely on self-administered personality tests.

The objectives of personality tests are an assessment of character traits and personality factors. They are intended to be useful to the individual concerned as they show which traits are strongly represented in the person's make-up

---

1 Begley T. M. and Boyd D. P., 'Psychological Characteristics Associated With Entrepreneurial Performance', Frontiers of Entrepreneurship Research, 1986, Babson College, Mass., USA.

and which are not. My particular favourite is the following. Answer *yes* or *no* to the following questions, keeping count:

Are you below average height?
Are you attractive to the opposite sex?
Have you ever broken speed limits?
Have you ever fiddled your taxes?
Are you a member of a minority group? (women answer *yes*)
Are you of an oppressed ethnic minority?
Are you always right?
Do you not suffer fools at all, let alone gladly?
Are you impatient?
Do you avoid taking advice?

If the number of *yes* answers is:

- between 0 and 2, you are probably better off (staying) in the civil service
- between 3 and 5, there is some chance for you,
- between 6 and 8, then you will probably make a reasonable entrepreneur
- more than 8, stay in the job, Prime Minister!

This simple test tells you very little beyond what you probably already knew, but it is often helpful to remind yourself of qualities within yourself – qualities which can be suppressed under the normal circumstances of your day-to-day life.

For further assessment, I include an excellent and more practical self-rating questionnaire. It was developed by Drs L. M. Spencer and R. Mansfield[1] and is reproduced with thanks.

It consists of 70 short statements. You read each statement and judge the degree to which the statement describes you. If it describes you very well, you grade it 5 and if it does not describe you at all, you grade it 1. This scale, developed by you, is then scored and your strength on thirteen different competencies is calculated. Competencies in this context would mean things like initiative and persistence. A full list is prepared later in the book. Be honest with yourself – no-one does everything well, nor should they want to.

Read each statement and grade it according to how well it describes you, using the following grades:

1 – not at all
2 – very little

---

1 Spencer L. M. and Mansfield R., 'The Identification And Assessment Of Competencies And Other Personal Characteristics Of Entrepreneurs In Developing Countries' Appendices for final Report, McBer & Co., 137 Newbury St., Boston, USA.

3 – somewhat
4 – well
5 – very well

Write the grade you give it in the space provided at the right hand side of the statement, grading all statements. Do it now and read how to score it afterwards.

1. I look for things that need to be done. ＿＿＿
2. I like challenges and new opportunities. ＿＿＿
3. When faced with a difficult job, I spend a lot of time trying to find a solution. ＿＿＿
4. When starting a new job or project, I gather a great deal of information. ＿＿＿
5. It bothers me when things are not done very well. ＿＿＿
6. I give much effort to my work. ＿＿＿
7. I find ways to do things faster. ＿＿＿
8. I plan a large project by breaking it down into smaller tasks. ＿＿＿
9. I think of unusual solutions to problems. ＿＿＿
10. I feel confident that I will succeed at whatever I try to do. ＿＿＿
11. I tell others when they have not performed as expected. ＿＿＿
12. I get others to support my recommendations. ＿＿＿
13. I develop strategies to influence others. ＿＿＿
14. No matter who I'm with, I'm a good listener. ＿＿＿
15. I do things that need to be done before being asked to by others. ＿＿＿
16. I prefer activities that I know well and with which I am comfortable. ＿＿＿
17. I try several times to get people to do what I would like them to do. ＿＿＿
18. I seek the advice of people who know a lot about the problems or tasks I am working on. ＿＿＿
19. It is important to me to do a high quality job. ＿＿＿
20. I work long hours and make personal sacrifices to complete jobs on time. ＿＿＿
21. I am not good at using my time well. ＿＿＿
22. I think about the advantages and disadvantages of different ways of accomplishing things. ＿＿＿
23. I think of many new ideas. ＿＿＿
24. I change my mind if others disagree with me. ＿＿＿
25. If I am angry or upset with someone, I tell that person. ＿＿＿
26. I convince others of my ideas. ＿＿＿
27. I do not spend much time thinking about how to influence others. ＿＿＿
28. I feel resentful when I don't get my own way. ＿＿＿

29. I do things before it is clear that they must be done. ____
30. I notice opportunities to do new things. ____
31. When something gets in the way of what I am trying to do, I keep on trying to accomplish what I want. ____
32. I take action without seeking information. ____
33. My own work is better than that of other people I work with. ____
34. I do whatever it takes to complete a job. ____
35. It bothers me when my time is wasted. ____
36. I try to think of all the problems I may encounter and plan what to do if each problem occurs. ____
37. Once I have selected an approach to solving a problem, I do not change that approach. ____
38. When trying something difficult or challenging, I feel confident that I will succeed. ____
39. It is difficult for me to order people to do things. ____
40. I get others to see how I will be able to accomplish what I set out to do. ____
41. I get important people to help me accomplish my goals. ____
42. In the past, I have had failures. ____
43. I take action before it is clear that I must. ____
44. I try things that are very new and different from what I have done before. ____
45. When faced with a major difficulty, I quickly go on to other things. ____
46. When working on a project for someone, I ask many questions to be sure I understand what the person wants. ____
47. When something I have been working on is satisfactory I do not spend extra time trying to make it better. ____
48. When working on a project for someone, I make a special effort to make sure that person is satisfied with my work. ____
49. I find ways to do things for less cost. ____
50. I deal with problems as they arise, rather than spend time trying to anticipate them. ____
51. I think of many ways to solve problems. ____
52. I do things that are risky. ____
53. When I disagree with others, I let them know. ____
54. I am very persuasive with others. ____
55. In order to reach my goals, I think of solutions that benefit everyone involved in a problem. ____
56. There have been occasions when I took advantage of someone. ____
57. I wait for direction from others before taking action. ____
58. I take advantage of opportunities that arise. ____
59. I try several ways to overcome things that get in the way of reaching my goals. ____

60. I go to several different sources to get information to help with tasks or projects. _____
61. I want the company I own to be the best of its type. _____
62. I do not let my work interfere with my family or personal life. _____
63. I get the most I can out of the money I have to accomplish a project or task. _____
64. I take a logical and systematic approach to activities. _____
65. If one approach to a problem does not work, I think of another approach. _____
66. I stick with my decisions even if others disagree strongly with me. _____
67. I tell people what they have to do, even if they do not want to do it. _____
68. I cannot get people who have strong opinions or ideas to change their minds. _____
69. I get to know people who may be able to help me reach my goals. _____
70. When I don't know something, I don't mind admitting it. _____

Having now graded each statement you can score the test. Enter each rating from the completed questionnaire on the lines above the statement number (which are in brackets under each line). Notice that the statement number in each column is consecutive: statement No 2 is below statement No 1, etc.

In each score there are five statements which have to be added or subtracted from one another depending on which signs are in the score. In each case 6 is added to the sum of the five grades to arrive at a score for each of the thirteen competencies being tested which are shown at the right hand side of the score. Add up the score to a total. Work out the correction factor in the same way as the other scores, except this time you add 18 to the sum of the grades to arrive at a score.

Scoring sheet for self-rating questionnaire

	Ratings of Statements				Score	Competency
_____ + _____ + _____ + _____ − _____ + 6 = _____						Initiative
(1) (15) (29) (43) (57)						
_____ − _____ + _____ + _____ + _____ + 6 = _____						Sees & Acts on Opportunities
(2) (16) (30) (44) (58)						
_____ + _____ + _____ − _____ + _____ + 6 = _____						Persistence
(3) (17) (31) (45) (59)						
_____ + _____ − _____ + _____ + _____ + 6 = _____						Information Seeking
(4) (18) (32) (46) (60)						

___ + ___ + ___ − ___ + ___ + 6 = ___ Concern for High Quality
(5)   (19) (33) (47) (61)   of Work

___ + ___ + ___ + ___ − ___ + 6 = ___ Commitment to Work
(6)   (20) (34) (48) (62)   Contract

___ − ___ + ___ + ___ + ___ + 6 = ___ Efficiency Orientation
(7)   (21) (35) (49) (63)

___ + ___ + ___ − ___ + ___ + 6 = ___ Systematic Planning
(8)   (22) (36) (50) (64)

___ + ___ − ___ + ___ + ___ + 6 = ___ Problem Solving
(9)   (23) (37) (51) (65)

___ − ___ + ___ + ___ + ___ + 6 = ___ Self-Confidence
(10) (24) (38) (52) (66)

___ + ___ − ___ + ___ + ___ + 6 = ___ Assertiveness
(11) (25) (39) (53) (67)

___ + ___ + ___ + ___ − ___ + 6 = ___ Persuasion
(12) (26) (40) (54) (68)

___ − ___ + ___ + ___ + ___ + 6 = ___ Use of Influence Strategies
(13) (27) (41) (55) (69)

TOTAL SCORE   ___

___ − ___ − ___ − ___ + ___ + 18 = ___ Correction Factor
(14) (28) (42) (56) (70)

Because we often try to fool ourselves as well as others in the way we present ourselves to the world, this test has a number of statements which are designed to spot if you have consciously or subconsciously answered untruthfully. The total of your grades to the statements becomes a correction factor, which will have to be subtracted from the total score for each of the competence factors.

In the space provided on the next score diagram, put in the correction factor. The correction factor ranges from 0 to 7 based on the following. If your correction factor score is:

24 or 25   subtract 7 from each competency score
22 or 23   subtract 5 from each competency score
20 or 21   subtract 3 from each competency score
19 or less subtract 0 from each competency score

Corrected score sheet

Competency	Original Score	−	Correction Number	=	Corrected Total
Initiative	___		___		___
Sees & Acts on Opportunities	___		___		___

Persistence	—	—	—
Information Seeking	—	—	—
Concern for High Quality of Work	—	—	—
Commitment to Work Contract	—	—	—
Efficiency Orientation	—	—	—
Systematic Planning	—	—	—
Problem Solving	—	—	—
Self-Confidence	—	—	—
Assertiveness	—	—	—
Persuasion	—	—	—
Use of Influence Strategies	—	—	—

CORRECTED TOTAL SCORE   —

Competency profile sheet for self-rating questionnaire

Instructions

1. Transfer the corrected competency score to the profile sheet by marking an 'X' at the appropriate point on the dotted horizontal line for each competency.

2. Draw a heavy line over the dotted horizontal line for each competency, from the left vertical line to the point you have marked with an 'X'. The heavy lines you have drawn graphically represent the strength of each competency.

3. The following is an example of how to create the profile sheet.

If the score for Initiative is 19, it will appear as follows:

Initiative ══════════════════════════════X--------------

      0   5   10   15   20   25

Profile sheet

Competency
Initiative   -

Sees and Acts
on Opportunities   -

Persistence   -

Information
Seeking   -

	0	5	10	15	20	25
Concern for High Quality of Work						
Commitment to Work Contract						
Efficiency Orientation						
Systematic Planning						
Problem Solving						
Self-Confidence						
Assertiveness						
Persuasion						
Use of Influence Strategies						

If you are uncertain how to continue after the initial gradings, the following example of my own score should help. I have already put my grades into the scoring sheet and worked out my scores, as follows:

Scoring sheet for self-rating questionnaire

Ratings of Statements   *Score*   *Competency*

$$\frac{3}{(1)} + \frac{3}{(15)} + \frac{3}{(29)} + \frac{3}{(43)} - \frac{3}{(57)} + 6 = \underline{15} \quad \text{Initiative}$$

$$\frac{4}{(2)} - \frac{4}{(16)} + \frac{4}{(30)} + \frac{3}{(44)} + \frac{4}{(58)} + 6 = \underline{17} \quad \text{Sees \& Acts on Opportunities}$$

$$\frac{3}{(3)} + \frac{4}{(17)} + \frac{3}{(31)} - \frac{3}{(45)} + \frac{3}{(59)} + 6 = \underline{16} \quad \text{Persistence}$$

$$\frac{3}{(4)} + \frac{4}{(18)} - \frac{3}{(32)} + \frac{2}{(46)} + \frac{3}{(60)} + 6 = \underline{15} \quad \text{Information Seeking}$$

$$\frac{4}{(5)} + \frac{4}{(19)} + \frac{4}{(33)} - \frac{3}{(47)} + \frac{5}{(61)} + 6 = \underline{20} \quad \text{Concern for High Quality of Work}$$

$$\frac{4}{(6)} + \frac{4}{(20)} + \frac{2}{(34)} + \frac{2}{(48)} - \frac{1}{(62)} + 6 = \underline{17}$$ Commitment to Work Contract

$$\frac{4}{(7)} - \frac{4}{(21)} + \frac{4}{(35)} + \frac{4}{(49)} + \frac{4}{(63)} + 6 = \underline{18}$$ Efficiency Orientation

$$\frac{5}{(8)} + \frac{5}{(22)} + \frac{4}{(36)} - \frac{2}{(50)} + \frac{3}{(64)} + 6 = \underline{21}$$ Systematic Planning

$$\frac{3}{(9)} + \frac{4}{(23)} - \frac{2}{(37)} + \frac{3}{(51)} + \frac{4}{(65)} + 6 = \underline{18}$$ Problem Solving

$$\frac{4}{(10)} - \frac{3}{(24)} + \frac{4}{(38)} + \frac{3}{(52)} + \frac{4}{(66)} + 6 = \underline{18}$$ Self-Confidence

$$\frac{3}{(11)} + \frac{3}{(25)} - \frac{4}{(39)} + \frac{2}{(53)} + \frac{3}{(67)} + 6 = \underline{13}$$ Assertiveness

$$\frac{3}{(12)} + \frac{2}{(26)} + \frac{2}{(40)} + \frac{3}{(54)} - \frac{4}{(68)} + 6 = \underline{12}$$ Persuasion

$$\frac{4}{(13)} - \frac{2}{(27)} + \frac{3}{(41)} + \frac{3}{(55)} + \frac{4}{(69)} + 6 = \underline{18}$$ Use of Influence Strategies

TOTAL SCORE   218

$$\frac{4}{(14)} - \frac{2}{(28)} - \frac{1}{(42)} - \frac{1}{(56)} + \frac{2}{(70)} + 18 = \underline{20}$$ Correction Factor

As you can see, I do delude myself to a certain extent and hence I have a correction factor of 3. The corrected scores are shown below:

CORRECTED SCORE SHEET

Competency	Original Score	− Correction Number	= Corrected Total
Initiative	15	3	12
Sees & Acts on Opportunities	17	3	14
Persistence	16	3	13
Information Seeking	15	3	12
Concern for High Quality of Work	20	3	17
Commitment to Work Contract	17	3	14
Efficiency Orientation	18	3	15
Systematic Planning	21	3	18
Problem Solving	18	3	15

37

Self-Confidence	18	3	15
Assertiveness	13	3	10
Persuasion	12	3	9
Use of Influence Strategies	18	3	15
	CORRECTED TOTAL SCORE		179

Finally, I have mapped the scores onto the profile sheet.

Profile sheet

Competency

Initiative

Sees and Acts
on Opportunities

Persistence

Information
Seeking

Concern for High
Quality of Work

Commitment to
Work Contract

Efficiency
Orientation

Systematic
Planning

Problem
Solving

Self-Confidence

Assertiveness

Persuasion

Use of Influence
Strategies

0   5   10   15   20   25

As you can see, the profile illustrates fairly middle-of-the-road results, with low scores on initiative and assertiveness, but a reasonably high score on systematic planning.

Now that you have a profile of your character based on the thirteen competencies, what exactly can you do with it? It gives you guidelines about what businesses are going to be suitable for you. Traits are only strong or weak in relation to the business (or job, or relationship) that you plan to operate, so having a high or a low score is irrelevant until you place it in the context of the tasks which have to be performed. Take my profile: I have a reasonably high score on systematic planning, and therefore might do quite well in businesses in which this is a strength – most of them, in fact. But the fact that I score highly on systematic planning is irrelevant to such businesses as scrap-metal dealing, popular music promotion, or foreign exchange dealing where this trait is of little value.

The fact that I seem to lack initiative would imply that I had better stick to businesses I already know something about. Because I seem to lack assertiveness, it's implied that I would not make a good self-employed insurance salesman, but might make good funeral parlour owner. Expressed another way, when evaluating an idea, try to see which of the thirteen competencies your idea would need a lot of and which only a little, and then measure yourself against these criteria.

Conclusion

Whatever your beliefs are regarding the right character traits, do not be discouraged; it is perfectly possible to find lots of people who one would have thought had the wrong personality for the successful running of a business. One of the most important personality traits is determination – if you are sufficiently determined to develop your own business, you will, no matter what your other characteristics may be.

Chapter Three
Common Reasons for Failure

Introduction

Over 100,000 businesses go bust, or otherwise out of business, each year. This is certainly proof enough that your own business makes heavy demands on you. The risks are extremely high – people lose their savings, homes, wives and families. You have got to get it right first time – very few people have two chances. This chapter is not intended to be negative – a discussion about failure before you have even started. However, there are some fairly common reasons for failing. Some of the failure factors can be avoided by an appropriate choice of business. For example, undercapitalization is often a cause of failure. Many firms fail through not having enough start-up money. If you do not have much money then you need to generate business ideas which do not stretch your resources; for instance window cleaning rather than manufacturing a new style of sports car in Northern Ireland. The most common reasons for failure are as follows:

- lack of knowledge of what is involved in the chosen business
- failure to understand the marketplace
- over-estimating sales
- launch delays
- too little money
- bad financial management
- getting the 'people bit' wrong

Knowing what the most common reasons are for the downfall of many companies can help you in avoiding these pitfalls yourself. It can help you to add constraints to your own framework – if you find dealing with people hard, then you can choose a type of business which does not need that particular skill. To allow you to work out if you need to add any constraints this way, look in more detail at the reasons for failure.

Lack of knowledge of what is involved in the chosen business

Many people start businesses with which they have no experience and thus have a fundamental lack of knowledge of what is involved in the chosen business. This can be a recipe for disaster. You will have heard of people who have made a success of such businesses. It is true that some people can and do attempt something absolutely foreign to anything they might previously have done. However, before you do jump into something you are less than knowledgeable about, ask them how they did it. Most will reply that it was luck – at least in the early stages.

Much of the research in the area of new businesses suggests that most men who start a business do so on the basis of earlier experience. It would appear that half the women who start businesses have no prior experience (but this also means that half do). Not having relevant experience handicaps you in the marketplace. You can easily be taken for a ride because you simply do not know better.

> Sue Herbert runs a delicatessen in Bedford called Bon Appetit. Her sole previous experience had been in accounts offices. When she started, she took on premises in a new shopping precinct – primarily on the basis of what the agent had told her. She felt she was lucky to have got the premises and was grateful to the agent. She came to a programme at Cranfield three months later and her major problem revolved around the fact that she simply did not have enough passing trade in her area of the precinct. We all spent many hours trying to dream up mechanisms that would increase the throughput traffic in her division – some successful, some not. At that time, Sue just did not have the experience necessary to tell her that what looked an excellent proposition was initially lousy for her business. It really was touch and go as to whether the business would survive long enough to enjoy its first anniversary.

So have you got the necessary experience? If you want to start a welding business immediately, you had better already know how to weld! This implies that you would be mad to start a business in an area where you have no experience. This is not entirely true – you would be merely handicapped in relation to everyone else in the marketplace, including the people who you are trying to earn an income from – your customers. Do not be disheartened, you can do something about it.

So how do you get the necessary experience? There are a number of ways of which the most important are the following:

- use the experience that someone else has already got, or
- get the experience yourself.

Using someone else's experience is not as difficult as it might sound. At its simplest, it may mean just buying in the skill – employing someone to round out your weaknesses. If you spot a grand opportunity for a Chinese Take-away anywhere, you should not let the fact that you cannot cook or you're not Chinese stop you. If you both can and are, your life will be simpler, it is true, but you can always employ people who can and are.

To look at it another way, you can use someone else's experience if they are your business partner (even better if they are also your domestic partner, because then you will not have to pay them). Partners can have major benefits: more money, theirs and your own; the necessary experience you need; a shared workload and more. Do be careful too, they also have major disadvantages: the absolutely fundamental need to trust each other; complementary, not duplicated skills; a workload irritatingly unequally shared; and obviously, a falling out between partners who are too emotionally close.

> Georgina Charnley is currently putting together a business plan for a company to be called 'Petscan'. It uses established human medical technology and hardware and applies it to pets. The scans will only get Veterinary approval if a qualified vet performs the work. As she is not a qualified Veterinarian her plans call for finding one who will go into partnership with her.

When I use the word partner most of you will be thinking of another like-minded individual – some partners could be other companies.

> Peter Saunders (yes, me) is currently working on an idea for a business which requires land-management skills and dealing with planning authorities, neither of which he possesses. The particular specialities that he needs almost certainly exist within National Car Parks Ltd. Unbeknownst to them (pre-publication), they will be on the receiving end of a proposal from him in the not too-distant future.

If NCP do take the idea up, it will be an example of 'Corporate Venturing' which is dealt with in Chapter 12.

The easiest, and almost certainly, best way of getting the experience for yourself is to work for someone else, preferably in the same industry. You may well have to delay your launch and make the sacrifice perhaps, of washing up in a wine bar – somewhat like the one you want to open.

> Sheila Halfyard wanted to set up a whole food shop. She had been a personnel manager beforehand and therefore took a large drop in status and more importantly, to my mind, money when, to further her ambition, she took a job as a sales assistant in a whole food shop not very far away from where she wanted to set up. During the two years she was there she learnt:
>
> - who the best suppliers were
> - what the best margin goods were
> - where the hot-spots were in a shop of this kind
> - what customers valued most
> - how to lay out a shop
> - what to expect in terms of sales
> - how to manage sales assistants
>
> Sheila also used those two years to find and set up her own ideal premises which she successfully moved into. Only eight weeks later she was breaking even – a phenomenal feat.

Actually, for Sheila, all was not coming up roses after the launch. She closed the business after only a few months because she found that she had not taken her own character into account. She is an extremely gregarious person and, although one meets a lot of different people in a retail outlet like hers, the most meaningful thing one ever gets to talk about is the weather. Sheila could have got round her problem by taking a partner or by hiring a manager but those actions simply were not in her vision and she did not choose to pursue them. Her dream was spoiled.

Failure to understand the marketplace

Product orientation

Too many people start businesses without any real idea of who will buy their product or service or why that customer should change from their existing sources of supply. Its easy to get very wrapped up with one's own idea and fail to take into consideration the most obvious keys to success. When we create a business based on products or services which have been generated from our ability to do something (rather than from an identified need in the marketplace) we normally have a 'product' approach to the business and this can blind us to the factors which operate within a marketplace, especially those which determine whether we succeed or fail. There is an old saying that: *'If you invent a better mousetrap the world will beat a path to your door.'*

Rubbish! You can invent any number of better mousetraps but no-one will come anywhere near your door until after you have told the world that a better mousetrap exists. It's important to be able to communicate with the world, a difficult task at the best of times. This means that you *have* to understand about advertising (which is communicating). Not only that but you have to promote the product in such a way that your claims are believable. Finally, given that the world is heavily dependent on convenience, no-one will come anywhere near your door until you make it easy for them to do so. What parking facilities do you have? Are you close to the M25?

The mousetrap syndrome seems to be especially true of people who set up retail outlets without prior experience. People will not just walk in from the street if you open your doors as a retailer. They have to have some thing to attract them through that door and tempt them to come back – time and time again. Generally, people are not sitting out there waiting to be sold to.

No market

People tend to simply assume that there will be a marketplace for their products.

> When Richard Farrar came back from a period of working in the Middle East he thought he would use his not inconsiderable savings opening a bike shop. He based the idea on his view that bicycle sales outlets seemed to be operating in the 19th Century. He found that there was absolutely no marketplace for his ideas in Bedfordshire or Cambridgeshire because people simply did not buy bicycles in the manner in which he was going to sell them.

Actually, Richard came to a programme at Cranfield before he set up and thus was able to make these mistakes on paper (market research and business planning) before setting up, saving himself a lot of money in the process. Richard used his personal framework to help evaluate the ideas he generated.

Applying his experience of the Middle East, he now runs a successful sales and marketing consultancy helping British firms sell their products.

Confusing features and benefits

Prospective businesspeople often confuse features and benefits. You, as a customer, buy benefits – the solutions to problems you have at a particular moment. Suppose for a moment that you are planning a holiday and want a simple camera to record the happier moments. You are interested in simplicity of operation, a camera that is capable of taking pictures in any conditions, easily available films/processing, and, perhaps, having the camera wind itself on to the next frame. It's unlikely that a sales pitch that concentrated on features like variable focal length from 24 to 70, 35mm or motor wind facilities which operate at 5 frames/second, would be successful or attractive to the potential buyer in this case.

> Doreen Jordan is an expert in the design of loud-speakers and has set up a company manufacturing high-quality miniature loudspeakers. Initially, her sales literature concentrated heavily on the technical details, written in the jargon which only sound scientists would understand, rather than the benefits – quality and size (written in terms that the layman would understand).

Not recognizing the difference between benefits and features can cause major problems, mostly in light of the fact that the customer has to work hard to glean information about the product or service being offered and *then* decide if it is for him. Naturally, this would make sales far more difficult.

Lack of segmentation

I mentioned earlier that you have to communicate with the world to let it know you have a better 'mousetrap'. In fact, there is no such thing a 'the world' when it comes to business. Few new business people recognize that humanity is not one homogenous mass. There are different groupings in humanity – each of which have different wants and needs. We call them segments, and a segment is a whole lot easier to deal with and, sell to than 'the world', en masse.

To take the mousetrap example, suppose you want to market these. Who, actually would be interested in using them? Youngsters? Unlikely, as the majority do not have separate households. Householders then? Yes, but even this is too wide – many people buy or rent newer housing which has less vermin problems than the older stock. OK – people who live in older properties? Probably, but does your mousetrap have the same attraction to people as owning a cat would? Right – people who live in older houses and who do not like cats? But hang on – your mousetrap costs four times as much as a traditional trap. Will the pensioners be able to afford it? Now, narrowed down even further, our potential customers would have to be people who live in older houses, do not like cats, and who have a disposable income beyond that of a state pension.

We are now beginning to get somewhere. You can probably refine the segmentation process down further in this example should you want to. Well, at least you now know it would be a waste of money to advertise the mousetrap in magazines such as 'Cat Lovers' Times' or 'Teenybopper'! On a more serious note, segmentation can run along all sorts of different lines. The factors which describe your market could be demographic: that is, based upon such factors as age, gender, socio-economic group, etc. Or they could be geographically based: a market centred mainly in London, or (better still) Yorkshire. You might find it better to segment in terms of benefits, point out to your market that the same product has different benefits to different people. Take the All Terrain Bike (the adult BMX) which for some people is mostly just for fun, while it also satisfies other groups' needs for exercise, status or simply for transport (they are becoming increasingly common amongst bicycle delivery men and women).

> Ruth bought a business which provides a typing service. It was not until she had been running it for some eighteen months that she realized that her customers had one factor in common: they all needed typing done as quickly as possible. In other words, her business had to have the same 'on call' facilities that an emergency breakdown service like the AA or the RAC had. She had been trying to sell her service through promoting quality. Through understanding segmentation it became obvious that her message must be speed and reliability; or, 'when all else fails, we can do it for you fast'.

Even where new business people do understand about the existence of segments they sometimes fall down on their choice of segment. Any segment should be measurable, accessible and sufficiently large to support a business.

Wrong location

The classical marketing error many people make is in the location of the business. Location is important for some ideas and not for others. What makes location important for your business? There are at least two factors to consider:

- do customers have to come to you?
- will you be relying on passing trade?

Shops and restaurants are usually in the latter group, although some do not rely on passing trade but on a reputation assiduously built up, in which case location is not as important. Many new retailers tend to go for cheap rentals and these properties are often on secondary shopping streets, condemning the business to a poor start. There are some factors one needs to consider regarding *any* possible site for a business:

- amount of traffic (pedestrian or automobile)
- parking
- visibility
- proximity to similar businesses
- the competitive advantage being sought
- ease of operation
- conversion
- cost

Even if this means that a lot more money has to be raised, it is preferable to have a location which is decided by the business needs rather than by whims or convenience. 'This space is available let's use it' is not a bugle call to success. However you may want to use a specific location (like your home), but remember that this in turn becomes a constraint which will have to be taken into account in the personal framework that you will be using to evaluate ideas. Your home town is a good place to start looking for prospective locations because that is where your location knowledge is best. It is also easier to get to work.

Over-estimating sales

Over-estimating sales forecasts boils down to having an overly rosy view of the likely results of the early trading. There are three basic reasons why new business people might do this: over-optimism about market size, underestimating the time needed to build up sales, and too little understanding of the selling process.

Over-optimism about market size

You can be over-optimistic for a number of reasons, the most common of which is thinking that your product or service is of interest to people in general – in other words failing to segment effectively.

Underestimating the time needed to build up sales

Many businesses rely on sales generated through sales calls on customers. Where this is the case it can take a very long time to reach the point at which one actually *makes* a sale. Even if a business starts trading in the High Street and thus is usually relying on passing trade, it will take some weeks for the passing populace to appreciate fully that a new outlet has been created. If a business has to rely on word of mouth as its sole promotional tool then it will need very patient owners (a trait not commonly noted amongst entrepreneurs).

Too little understanding of the selling process

In most cases it is you who will be doing the selling, especially in the early stages. Many people simply have no understanding of the selling process – how much time it will take, what can be done in a day, how many selling days there are, etc. I often meet people who come out with statements like 'I will have to sell £250,000 to make sufficient profits for my needs' without considering the implications of this from a selling and operational point of view. They just do not take on board the practical aspects of selling. For example:

> Howard Fabian came on a course at Cranfield a few years ago to develop and market a see-through greeting card. His largest markets are London and South East where there are 120 solid customers. He worked out that he could make 4–5 calls a day and thus he needed 4–5 weeks to get round them all. He also needed to continue to service the best 30 customers every month – the next best 30 every 2 months and the other 60 he would cover by phone, post (new designs) and occasional visits. This leaves him only 5 days a month for all the other aspects of his business, including finding new customers.

In actuality, this outline assumes that Howard works only a five day week. If he did he would not be in business for long as the other aspects of Howard's business do take up much more than his 5 extra days a month. Naturally, like most people who run their own businesses, he uses the time that many working people consider sacrosanct – their evenings and weekends. Retail outlets need planning in terms of time, too:

> Matt and Tessa were planning to launch a fast food outlet. They planned to have only themselves and one other person working in the unit, which would be open 9 am to 9 pm, six days a week: a total of 72 hours. With an hour to open and another to close up, and the opening hours they were planning, everyone connected with the business would have been totally exhausted by the end of the first week. They were even planning to be there all the time themselves. Eventually they realized that more staff would be necessary.

Launch delays

The failure to appreciate how long it takes to launch a business can be the ruin of it. It is my experience that if you take your original estimates and multiply them by 5 you will not be far off. Where the business's location is important to subsequent sales performance it can take even longer because the premises search and decision become vital and time-consuming activities:

> Matt and Tessa had planned to launch their fast food outlet in the Spring of 1987. They had contacted British Rail and London Transport to try to get an outlet in a station concourse. They had seen the major letting agents for the Oxford Street Plaza and the other large shopping developments. They eventually launched their fast food business, 'Froghurt', in the Gateshead Metrocentre in August of 1988.

But some businesses naturally take longer to set up than others:

> Leo Montoute, Andy Burnett and Ian Pearson developed an idea for a 'Report Outliner' in their final year of university in early 1986. Their product, called

Clarity, is a piece of computer software designed to help one write reports and other matters more effectively. In July 1988 they had only just one Beta Test version out – the version that they can give to people to practise with to enable them to iron out any final bugs before launching the wonder product on the market.

It has taken nearly 7 man years of effort to get this software anywhere near a marketable state, although the business end of the product – the outliner itself – was ready two years ago.

Too little money

To start a business you need money for two things:

- to set up the business so that it can physically trade
- to cover the costs of trading until the business becomes self supporting

The first is usually called 'start-up costs' or just 'capital', and the second, 'working capital'. Running out of either can seriously damage your health – or business health, at least, and new business people regularly damage both.

Start up costs too high

Any new business, from the smallest to the largest, will incur start-up costs; at the very minimum the business will need some stationery, probably designed specifically for the firm (if the business wants to look professional). At the other end of the scale look at Graham Smith:

Graham, using his long experience as a manager and engineer in the ceramics trade, is setting up a factory to manufacture replicas of Victorian toilets. He needs land to build the factory or a ready-built unit. In either event he is budgeting some £1 million. He then needs to hire a workforce who will probably have to be trained. Their first task is to build the two kilns that the business will need (hence the possible need for a specially built factory). His budget for this is £0.5 million. He needs other plant equipment totalling £0.5 million. This is all before he has begun to plan for such necessities as the reps' cars or the office fixtures and fittings.

New retailers and restaurateurs often simply forget how expensive conversion of the premises can be, especially when going for a specific corporate identity.

> Edmund Bradley's first pick-and-mix sweet outlet, called Jamboree, is in Hamley's Birmingham store. The largest component of a £30,000 fittings cost was the £15,000 design fee.

There are usually dozens of things which have to be considered: from the lease premium costs and associated legal fees (did you know that you very often have to pay the lessors legal fees as well as your own?) to the coffee machine. Underestimating the start up costs can have only three outcomes:

- You have to get more money from somewhere. This can lead you into going on bended knee to your financial backers, which at the very least is going to be embarrassing and at the worst, fruitless.
- You raid the money you had set aside for working capital, often with consequently disastrous results (*see below*).
- You go out of business at this juncture.

Obviously, you might be sufficiently wealthy to draw a little more from your investments, but in general, entrepreneurs do suffer from lack of financing.

Lack of working capital

Lack of working capital can be as bad for you as running out of money to start the business. When you start a business you may well need to have *some* stocks of goods at the very minimum – this is especially true for retailers or anyone else who sells a physical product as opposed to providing a service. These stocks cost money, and cost money before you have had the chance to sell the goods concerned.

If you plan to sell on credit, and there are few businesses which do not, especially if their customers are other businesses, it could easily take three months or longer to get the money back. Meanwhile, you have paid out for the materials and labour involved in that sale. This all costs money. You may need to advertise or incur other promotional costs before you make a sale. Again, this costs money. Having too little working capital means that you restrict your sales, possibly with disastrous consequences:

The new owner, who will remain nameless, of the little off-licence and grocer round the corner from my country place had too little money left, after buying the shop, to invest in a reasonably full range of products. He told me that as soon as the sales started to pick up he would be able to get a better range. Sales never did pick up because he never had the things people wanted – there were large holes in his stock. It got to the stage that he started acting like Uriah Heep when anyone came in the shop so as to encourage them to come back again – which they did not do because they felt uncomfortable. It's easy to identify a shop going downhill and, as a customer, you want no part of it. The only time he made sales was when the other shops were closed, which was not a great deal of the time. The shop is now shuttered but he still lives there. Not surprisingly, he was unable to find a buyer.

This is a very sad tale, especially for someone who has seen him go from an optimistic, ebullient and pleasant man to one who is a semi-recluse whose dreams, savings and livelihood have been shattered. But it all stems from having insufficient working capital. Oddly enough, too great success early on can also put major pressures on your working capital. This is called 'over-trading'.

Over-trading

I hope that all people who start businesses have potential over-trading problems because it means that, on the selling front, they are doing something right. An example of this situation is the Snedkers.

Jim and Bob Snedker had been in business selling 'in-line' printers to polythene bag manufacturers for about 7 months when they received an order for 15 units from a Belgian customer. Each machine costs roughly £4,000 in materials, with another £2,000 going in labour. Bob and Jim could have simply started to fill the order without increased financial aid but they would have had the bank manager bouncing cheques within 6 weeks, and consequently, would have had to close down. The problem they faced was that to build the 15 machines they have to find £90,000 for the materials and labour long before they ever would ever get the money from the Belgians.

Bob and Jim were on a Cranfield course at the time and they had learnt to apply a technique called 'cash flow forecasting' to their business, and thus they spotted the likely cash deficiency before it arose. Before the crisis is the best time for managing cash flow problems. Your alternatives for handling a cash crisis after it has arisen are severely limited; whereas, if you can see it coming, you have, possibly, hundreds of ways of dealing with it.

Over-trading is only a problem only if it creeps up unnoticed. There are certain techniques (not the subject matter of this book) which can help you avoid such problems.

Bad financial management

Not everyone has the benefit of twenty years as an accountant (luckily for them, some would say) and must have very few financial skills when they start a business. This is a pity, in many respects, as it can lead just as surely to the downfall of a great idea as all the other reasons given above. There are two basic reasons why people's lack of financial management skills is important to the continued success or otherwise of the idea: mistaking cash for profit, and having no management accounts available.

Mistaking cash for profit

When a business starts there is both money coming in and money going out. If the money coming in is bigger than the money going out than there are cash surpluses. Quite often these surpluses get mistaken for profit, which, more often than not, they are not.

For example, suppose you set up a business selling a subscription only magazine. In the first month you receive 200 annual subscriptions at £12 each, a cash receipt of £2,400. Suppose also that it costs £100 to produce the first month's magazines and another £50 in overheads for the month, cash payments totalling £150. You would have a cash surplus for the month, so:

	£
Receipts	2,400
Payments	150
Cash surplus	2,250

But cash surpluses are not profits. Your profit for the month is only:

	£
Income (one month's subscriptions)	200
Expenses	150
Profit	50

If you had mistaken cash for profit in the first month, you could easily have spent the whole of the cash surplus of £2,250, leaving yourself with cash difficulties in later months.

In this example, the distinction between cash and profits is fairly easy to see, but this is not always true of all businesses. In addition to using the cash flow forecasts mentioned earlier, you also need to estimate what your profit will be.

No management accounts

When any business operates it has outcomes which can usually be measured in terms of money. Far too many people who start businesses deprive themselves of a lot of very useful information by leaving the preparation of the accounts to the accountant at the end of the year. How would your enjoyment of cricket, football, snooker or any other game be affected by having to wait until the game had finished before the score was announced? The players themselves would be more than somewhat handicapped by such a situation. It is therefore important to keep on top of and in touch with your profit position at all times. The end of your financial year is often too late to readjust a waning position.

Getting the 'people bit' wrong

Most businesses that reach any size involve more people than just the owner. You need to ask yourself if you can handle people because if you cannot you need to find an idea that does not involve many of them.

> Kendall Chew runs a company called Bullet Couriers. One of Kendall's competitive edges is the presentation and attitude of his staff. In consequence he recruits reasonably well-educated delivery people and provides vans, rather than bikes. Managing his workforce is very important to the success of his business.

Just the recruitment and selection of your prospective employees requires a great deal of careful forethought. It is essential to define your needs with every step you take. The subsequent management of people can be a horror show for those not experienced in such things. The motivation of your employees in terms of your ethics and working style is going to be a major job. At the very minimum, expectations differ between owner and employee. Owners generally would like 80 hours of work for 40 hours' pay (a feat most enterprises must handle), but employees are more likely to want 20 hours' work for 40 hours' pay. You also need to get the working environment right – sweat shops are, by and large, out of the question nowadays.

The recruitment, selection and subsequent management can be a costly and time-consuming process. Getting rid of the wrong people for your firm, even if they are not protected by employment rights under statute, can be extremely difficult, and often because you might have been getting on well with the individual concerned – on a personal level. Again, you are their source of income, with most people, their only source. They depend on you and you should not take that responsibility lightly. There are several factors to consider when assessing the employment aspects and implications of an idea:

- how many employees will you need, and of what type – must they be skilled?
- the availability of the types of labour you need
- skill levels – will they need *much* training (they will always need *some*, even if only a short indoctrination in your business ethics and way of doing things).
- safety
- working environment

In fact, this book cannot even attempt to outline the multiplicity of different things to consider when employing. Human resources management is a vast and often tricky subject to deal with. I can suggest an excellent source of further information: The Small Business Guide, CGT Barrow, BBC Publications.

Conclusion

Some of these factors are dealt with in more detail in Part III of this book, specifically those dealing with the marketing aspects of the proposed product or service. The reasons for failure are useful in helping you develop a personal framework to generate and evaluate business ideas which would be attractive for you (see Chapter 5).

Chapter Four
Common Types of Business

Introduction

Just as there are common reasons for failure, there are also common types of business. Different types of business have different characteristics that are important in deciding whether a particular idea will suit you. This chapter outlines the advantages and disadvantages of some of the more common types of businesses to help you understand the implications of your choice of idea on your lifestyle.

Catering

> Charles and Daniel came to a course at Cranfield to help them set up their own restaurant. They did this, setting it up in Richmond Upon Thames and calling it The Culinary Art Company. They discovered many factors in their experiences which would be of help to you in understanding what is involved.

Start up costs

Start up costs tend to be high. Charles and Daniel went for a high street location which meant they had to pay a premium (the purchase price of leased properties). Reasonable properties in high streets (outside London) go for anything between £30,000 and £100,000 just to purchase. On top of that sum you have the costs of conversion, where necessary, and the fixtures and fittings. All told, another £30,000 to £100,000 is required.

Margins

Charles and Daniel found that the business has good margins – they could usually charge 100% in mark-up on the cost of booze, and 67% on the cost of food. However, in common with other restaurateurs, they found that their restaurant is rather expensive to run. Restaurant wages can be anything between 25% to 33% of sales revenue and the costs of heat, light and power are not inconsiderable.

Skills needed?

Generally, experience with other similar ventures is needed – you must have your own experience or access to the necessary experience by buying it in. Too many people start catering outlets without really knowing what is involved, often simply on the basis of the fact that they enjoy cooking or have an image of themselves as 'le Patron'. If you want set up an outlet because you enjoy cooking, go and get a job as a short-order chef for a place catering for two or three hundred meals a day just to see how short-lived your enjoyment could be.

Lifestyle effects

The whole business is extremely tiring – with long hours and little outside social life.

Hotels

> John and Sally Boycott decided they would buy a hotel to satisfy their desire to run their own business. John's entire career had been in promotional work for large organizations and Sally was a surveyor. They came across an opportunity on the south coast and went ahead and bought it.

They are just now, six months in, coming to realize that there is a lot more to running even a small hotel than they had initially imagined. Although running a hotel is very interesting with lots of variety, it is also very tough work – seasonal, often very busy, and, worst of all, a hotel never closes. The Boycotts are on call 24 hours a day, 365 days a year.

Start-up costs

There is a high start-up cost, whether you buy a hotel or convert a building into a hotel. John and Sally paid £350,000 for a relatively run-down operation and immediately spent a further £75,000 doing the place up to their satisfaction. If the proposition looks reasonable, finance is usually available in the form of commercial mortgages up to, say, 70% of the purchase price. John and Sally have a £200,000 mortgage, which means that they had to find £225,000 from their own resources. And all of this before finding the money to finance the day-to-day operations (working capital).

Margins

In the European Hotel (John and Sally's) there are three streams of income: letting rooms, their two bars, and the restaurant. The margins on the restaurant are very similar to those I outlined earlier in the Catering section, and can be quite high. Net profits on the bar operations are in the region of 15% of sales.

Skills needed?

The answer to whether or not you need specific skills to run a hotel is a definite *yes*. There is much involvement with customers, and you need patience, a sense of humour, and broad-mindedness. It really is not a job for anyone who cherishes privacy and you need to be a 'jack of all trades' – preferably all of them at once. It needs experience, preferably of a similar operation but if not, a knowledge of catering is an asset. You will need certain domestic abilities combined with versatility and flexibility. You must be somewhat restrained, because you can easily become over-involved, and over-involvement can be debilitating.

Even the smallest hotels need staff and you will be employing people from your first day. Consequently you need some people management skills. These skills are going to be very important as the success of any hotel is largely dependent on the relationships that the staff build up with customers. Think of your own experiences of hotels – it is not always the rooms or other facilities which distinguish a good hotel from a bad hotel in your mind.

The hotel industry is also rife with all sorts of imaginative rip-offs, including, amongst others, what the clothing retail industry has come to call 'shrinkage' (which I thought was what happened to my jeans when I washed them, but in fact is the theft of stock by employees and guests). This is where experience comes in very handy, because if you are aware of the many different ways that you can suffer 'shrinkage' or other dubious behaviour, you can probably do something about controlling it to some extent.

Lifestyle effects

As John and Sally are coming to realize, running a hotel does not just have 'lifestyle effects', it is lifestyle all of its own. It is very hard, often frustrating work, and highly demanding of your time. Your family is certain to be heavily affected. Even if your spouse is not going to work in the hotel, he or she will probably still be living there. They cannot get away from it any more than you can. Your children will have to put up with late nights, disturbed occasionally by the odd drunk, guest illnesses, unhappy clièntèle or staff – virtually anything can plague the evenings of a hotel owner.

Do not let all this deter you unnecessarily, for running a hotel can also be very personally satisfying, especially when the same customers keep coming back: the ultimate judgement of a hotelier's service.

Retailing

Starting a retail outlet is a very popular route to starting your own business. There is usually a lot less seasonality involved than, say, hotels. Retail outlets are not usually dependent on fickle popularity or the desire for 'something new' that can plague restaurants. (That does however, depend largely on what type of product is being sold.) If the product itself is a 'fashion' item then the shop is at risk from trend changes. It is however, obviously easier to change stock than it is to change menus or décor. They are, however, vulnerable to changes in their immediate environment because they depend so heavily on location to make them successful.

> Brenda Brewer and her daughter started a shop selling the lace-related products they had been producing for years as their hobby. They chose a secondary shopping street just off the high street and moved in. The choice of street is the factor which keeps their sales down – there simply is not enough passing trade to make the shop the success its products actually deserve.

There is a large market for buying and selling shops, so it is relatively easy to get into retailing even if you do not want to set up your own from scratch. Go to the commercial arm of the larger Estate Agents in your town if you want to see what is available near you. But beware people's reasons for selling (*see Chapter 9*).

Start-up costs

The amount of the start-up costs of a retail outlet will depend entirely on the type of business you begin. There are obviously differences between expecting your customers to come to you, as in a wine warehouse, or taking the business to where your customers currently shop, as in a clothing outlet. If you can realistically expect your customers to come to you, then you need a showroom and sufficient car parking space. The major benefit of such an operation is that you do not have to locate it in the centre of a town where property prices are higher. You may be able to pick up leases for just a few thousand pounds, with cheaper rental costs.

However, the sort of operation where customers are willing to come to you rather than the other way round are fairly few and far between. Some of the few operations are:

- anything to do with cars, as people will be using them anyway – for instance an exhaust centre.
- a large shed operation where you can offer convenience through a complete service for 'one stop' shopping (but the large size means that this would need quite a lot of capital, thus defeating the original reason for an out of centre location) – for example a garden centre or a DIY store.
- a 'specialist' outlet retailing otherwise unavailable goods or services – if you run the only place people can get the 'left hand screw zx188|gww/5mm' part that they need for whatever esoteric thing they are constructing – you are pretty much in demand, wherever you are located.

If the shop you are considering is not fortunate enough to have its customers come to you, then you will need a shopping centre location. Then the problem becomes one of deciding what quality of location you need. If you have to rely on passing trade then you need a location with a great deal of pedestrian traffic and these tend to be expensive. A good location in the shopping centre of towns outside London could be in the region of £50,000 to £100,000 for the premium with rentals of £30,000 p.a. Add another £25,000 to £50,000 to the price for reasonable London locations.

On top of all of this, you have conversion and fitting costs. The cost of these will depend on what type of outlet you are considering. Incidentally, I would far rather see anyone who wants to set up a shop go for the best high street locations, even though they are more expensive. It is difficult enough to ensure the success of a new retail outlet without compounding the problem by having to drum up trade from a dicky secondary position.

Margins

Margins in retailing could be anything, so it is difficult to give you a good idea of what is normal. For most *categories* there are reasonably standard rates, but the difficulty is that there are so many different categories of retailing. Here are examples of three:

- clothing – most retailers mark their prices by simply doubling their buy-in cost (meaning that their gross profits should be in the region of 50% of sales).
- groceries – again the retailers in this category have a simple method of arriving at prices: they add half their buy-in price to the cost, meaning that their gross profits should be in the region of 33% of sales.
- furniture – these retailers triple their buy-in price when they sell; therefore, their gross profits are about 67% of sales. A handsome margin, but with low volumes in number terms.

If you have no idea what to expect, go to talk to a retailer in another town who will feel safe that you are not in competition with him. There is nothing a small business person likes better than talking about his or her business because in the ordinary course of events they have no-one to talk to about it – aside from customers who generally waft in and back out again.

There is one financial point that is common to most retail outlets – sales are normally in cash. This can be a major benefit in terms of improving cash flows, because the supplies are often on credit and you may find yourself in the happy position of having had the cash for the goods before you have to pay for them, thus using someone else's money to help finance your business. Alternatively, however, it is sometimes more difficult to manage cash than money on paper.

Skills needed?

Yes, is still the answer to this question, but far less so than the earlier examples because a shop is comparatively simple to run. There are fewer skills necessary. However, all retailers have a very important aspect of their businesses, which they need to master – customers. How many times have you been in a shop recently where the person wanting to serve you has asked 'can I help you?' That question predicates its own answer: 'no thank you' or 'I am only looking, thanks'. You will need a certain modicum of selling skills – unusual approaches to the customers that still incorporate helpfulness, charm and most importantly, salesmanship.

Perhaps I should also plea that you get yourself some business skills too, because I do not want you, my reader, to be like so many other people, opening a shop and sitting back expecting people to walk in your door simply because you have opened it. You have to give people a reason for wanting to change to you from their existing supplier (*see Chapter 3*).

Lifestyle effects

There is little doubt that retailing like almost any entrepreneurial project is hard work. You are physically tied to the shop and can expect long hours with few or no holidays. And it can become excruciatingly boring, filling the hours when only a small number of people come in. Fortunately you can shut the shop, sometimes as early as 6pm, and you often have a day a week (Sunday) away from it – unlike hoteliers and many restaurateurs.

Service Businesses

It is extremely difficult to give a generalized picture of the service industry since there are so many and their natures are varied. Service businesses include such things as accountants, lawyers, building contractors, window cleaners, and many many others.

> Melanie Stoyel set up a bookkeeping and secretarial service, called Paperclear, operating from a small office in a building in Greenwich High Road, in South East London. The building was an old factory which a firm called Skillion had converted into nursery units: small units for new businesses, let on monthly licence. Melanie was one of the first businesses into the newly converted factory, and as it filled, it brought new customers to her.

Another example is that of Ray Harness:

> Ray set up a business specializing in painting industrial premises. Because he goes out to his clients rather than them coming to him, Ray can use his home as the base for the business.

In a similar vein:

> Ken and his brother David set up a business called Fox Glove Contracting (UK) Ltd., which concentrates on the demolition and removal of the dangerous types of asbestos. His biggest difficulty is not finding customers, or appropriate licences, but in locating sufficiently skilled labour.

David Thornton provides a service to manufacturers who want to have parts made by castings. He identifies his customer's problems and finds the most appropriate casting company to make up that part.

As you can see from these examples, service businesses can differ intensely. Ken's smallest contract is in the region of £75,000 and Melanie's largest invoices are rarely more than £75.00. There does, however, seem to be one factor in common in all four cases: the essence of the service business is the sale of expert labour.

Start-up costs

Given that the essence of the service business is the sale of expert labour, often just you, these types of businesses have the lowest start-up costs of all. You might be able to start up from your home, especially when the business is such that your customers do not come to you but you to them. Even when you do have to meet a client at your premises, it is perfectly possible to have arranged with the suppliers of accommodation addresses to hire an office for a few hours.

Where such alternatives are not available to you, it is still relatively cheap (when compared to such start-ups as buying a retail lease) to hire small offices on monthly terms in shared buildings, thus giving yourself a permanent, sometimes high quality, but always flexible, base from which to operate.

Warwick Executive Services rent out 200 square feet offices by the month in Birmingham and other parts of the Midlands. They provide a shared receptionist/telephonist and have arranged the telephone equipment in such a way that calls to their clients are separately identified, thus allowing the telephonist to answer the call in the client's own business name. In addition, when a customer or other visitor of their clients calls, there is nothing to show that the operation is a shared one between the clients and thus can enhance your professional and commercial image.

So you can start a service business on a shoestring – even as little as the cost of your commercial letterhead.

Margins

It is impossible to give you any real guidance on the margins of service businesses as they are dependant on your personal service: how expert and scarce the labour that you are selling is.

> David Thornton's first year's turnover was in the region of £28,000 and his net profit £19,000.
>
> Ken's margins in the asbestos demolition and removal trade are also high because there are few firms with the necessary skills or licences.
>
> Melanie's margins, however, are quite low because there are quite a few similar operations. While she can afford to charge a higher price than most of her competition because of her location, convenient hours and quality, she could not, say, triple her competitors' prices because in doing so she would go out of business.

Skills needed?

Again, given that the essence of the service business is the sale of expert labour, you need a skill itself or you need easy access to one, in terms of hiring it. There are two fundamental factors underlying the success of any service business, especially in its early days:

- the need to persuade potential customers that you can fulfil the promises you are making regarding what service it is you can provide
- fulfilling the promises – being able to provide the service professionally

Without the first ability you will not get any customers at all and without the second you will not get any satisfied customers. Satisfied customers are vital to the longer-term growth of the business because they become a selling tool for the first factor: persuading people what you can do for them. The service business cannot show or demonstrate to a prospective customer its goods to help the customer make up his or her mind because service is often intangible. However, when a service has satisfied customers, you can use these as models of your success.

As a result of, and in addition to having the skill yourself, you need the skill of being able to create confidence in the minds of others: you need the ability to sell yourself.

Lifestyle effects

It is impossible to give you any real guidelines because of the enormous variety of service businesses. Suffice to say that all new owners of businesses have a hard time: you have to live eat and breathe the business, and there is also the inevitable tension of the fact that your income is no longer as secure as it was.

Manufacturing

Like service businesses, there are a number of different types of manufacturing businesses, each with its own individual problems and success factors. So, here too, it is impossible to make a generalized statement that will encompass all the industries. Possible manufacturing businesses include making plastic toys, sofa beds, electronic wizardry, and all sorts of weird and wonderful things.

> Graham Eastland (G.E.) is currently manufacturing and selling a heat sensitive switch based on bi-metal strips. His business is not yet sufficiently large to afford any employees at all so Graham manufactures the product himself in his garage. He is also the chief (and only) salesperson.
>
> Graham Smith (G.S.) is currently in the process of setting up a factory to manufacture ceramic replicas of Victorian toilets (as mentioned in Chapter 3).

As difficult as it is to give a general view, I propose to contradict myself in the sense that all manufacturers do have two factors in common:

- making a physical product, and
- selling that product.

This means that all manufacturing businesses need:

- somewhere to manufacture: in G.E.'s case, his garage; and for G.S. a purpose-built factory in North West Wales.
- something to make the product with – in G.E.'s case, a bench and drill; and in G.S.'s case, two purpose-built kilns to fire the clay, moulds, and other pieces of equipment.
- material to make the product from: in G.E.'s case, bi-metal strip, some

cases, screws and other bits; in G.S.'s case, the raw clay, the glazes, the other fittings.
- a workforce to make the products: in G.E.'s case, himself; in G.S.'s case, an entire labour force who have to be trained and whose first real job will be building the kilns referred to earlier.
- a sales force to sell the product: in G.E.'s case, himself; in G.S.'s case, another entire group of people, including himself.

Start-up costs

Because of the wide variety of manufacturing businesses I cannot specify in exact terms what it might normally cost. You can see from the above two examples how disparate the start-up costs could be. If I tell you that G.E.'s start up costs were in the region of £2,500 but that G.S.'s were one thousand times bigger at £2,500,000, I doubt if you would be surprised. It really all depends on how ambitious your plans are.

Margins

Manufacturing businesses tend to have relatively low net profit to sales figures (a rough guesstimate would have it at 10%) but tend to have large volumes, so that their absolute profit figures (when not compared to sales revenue) can be quite large.

Skills needed?

The answer to this question *has* to be a resounding *yes*. Just look at what G.E.'s skills have to be to run even a small operation:

- he must be the buyer
- he has to be able to make the switch itself
- he has to be able to sell the switch

Add to those the skills that G.S. must accomplish:

- he is the property developer
- he has to know how to lay out factories that perform at maximum efficiency – getting that wrong with two very large purpose-built kilns would be disastrous
- he has to have major personnel skills
- he has to be a factory manager

- he has to manage a sales force – buying their cars and organizing their tasks
- he has to decide the best ways to finance the operation (the finance director's job)

All in all, manufacturing businesses are probably the most difficult to set up. This might explain why so few people bother – only some 6 – 10% of all new firms are manufacturing firms.

Lifestyle effects

If you plan to start a manufacturing business, be prepared for trying times – when technology is involved, it doesn't take long for things to go wrong. Beyond that, everything I noted about service businesses is true of manufacturing businesses.

Conclusion

This Chapter should have helped you to confirm what type of business interests you and also establish whether or not such a business is within your resources, in terms of money, mental make-up, and physical health. You can now build these factors into your personal framework.

Chapter Five:
Building a Personal Framework

Introduction

It is important for you to build a personal framework – one that is unique to you – because it can help in two areas:

- generating the ideas themselves
- evaluating ideas for their suitability from your own point of view.

While you are spending time looking at your objectives, yourself, and your character traits, you will automatically be thinking of why you are doing these tasks: ostensibly, to be able to launch your own business. In itself, this thought process *creates* business ideas. If you are looking for opportunities, the simple fact is that you have started seeing the world in a slightly different manner than you did a short time ago. It doesn't take long to find you asking yourself 'can I make a successful business out of that?' Building a personal framework helps that process because you will be able to go on to asking: 'how can I take advantage of that trait?' or 'what ideas fit in with this particular objective?'

In addition to helping you generate ideas, the framework acts as a measuring stick for the ideas as they are generated. You can test the ideas against the framework to see how well they fit with your objectives, traits and constraints. This is vital because ending up in a business that you are not really suited to can be soul destroying – you'll find yourself with no motivation, no enjoyment, the inability to move away, and so on. So far, if you have followed the suggestions in Chapters 1 and 2, you are in a position to be able to list your objectives, your constraints and your character competencies. You can now use these lists to help you create the framework to help your generation of ideas and the important tasks of filtering and evaluating the ideas.

Your Personal Framework

The framework is built out of the three major areas we looked at.

- where you want to go – your objectives
- the things which arrest your progress – your constraints
- what you personally are good or bad at – your character traits.

The end result will be a model which has the three dimensions: goals, constraints, and capabilities.

Objectives

If you have not already done so, list your objectives. You should have a number of different categories of goals, ranging from family matters to business matters, from long- to medium- and short-term goals. Within each category, place them on the list in the order of their importance to you. For example:

Do you remember Ray Roberts from chapter I? One of his long term goals is to be in the position of never having to worry about money again when he retires. For him this means an income, in today's terms, of $100,000 per annum for the rest of his life. Another of his long term objectives is to achieve control of his own destiny and consequently he was obliged, by his objectives, to start his own business: he founded a specialized market research company.

Take Ray's long term objectives: that of achieving a comfortable retirement income, and autonomy. To achieve them both he must sell his own successful business, or at least own one, at retirement. So his medium term goal is to own and operate a reasonably successful business. And his short-term goals are as follows:

- find an idea he would be happy with, one that has commercial opportunities
- research the idea
- get finance
- get premises
- resign from Rothmans
- launch a business

From this we can see that Ray's retirement income objective is more important than his autonomy goal because if it were not, the medium-term goal would read: owning and operating a business which provides a living, thus fulfilling the autonomy goal at the cost of the retirement income goal.

Setting up any business will mean compromising some of your objectives – no one business can hope to achieve them all. Go through your own objectives and put them in their order of importance to you.

Constraints

Similarly, list your constraints and place them in their order of importance. If you have not already done so, write down the list in the following categories:

- Income
- Time
- Family matters
- Support and motivation
- Resources
- Money
- People
- Materials
- Knowledge/experience/skills

Now reorder them into their relative positions according to your own personal situation.

Characteristics

You now have a list of thirteen competencies, some of which will have quite high scores and others, quite low scores. Simply re-order the competencies so that the one with the highest score comes first and the one with the lowest, last. For the moment, and until you reach the evaluation stage in Chapter 13, this is all you need do.

Using the framework

Compiling the framework should have helped to generate some ideas, which is really a 'spin-off' benefit because the framework's major use is in evaluation of ideas. Early evaluation of ideas can lead to the situation where you miss some excellent opportunities (*see Chapter 7*) so the best thing you can do with the framework right now is to put it aside until you have some ideas you want to evaluate and then you can use it as a filter (*see Chapter 13*).

PART II: IDEA GENERATION

The ability to generate ideas is not dependent on how creative a person is, as many people believe. Creativity is something which we all use every day of our lives, even if it is used in the form of a new short cut to work or a better way of doing a task when you get there. Idea generation is dependent, like most things in our lives, on how much effort one puts into it: the harder the work, the more ideas that result. And you do want large numbers of ideas:

- for every idea that gets implemented into a business there are 100 (or even 1000) ideas which are discarded;
- at this stage you are concerned with numbers rather than quality, which comes later.

Idea evaluation could be thought of as a sieving process, where raw ideas are put in the fine-meshed sieve, which allows only the workable ideas through. It follows, therefore, as with any sieve, that the more you pour in it, the more you will end up with. And the same applies to business ideas. Essentially there are two ways to come up with ideas for creating a business – generate your own, or develop someone else's.

The second of the two is by far the most common. In fact it could be argued that the first does not exist, and that every successful business is a development of an earlier business concept. For example:

> Anita Roddick, the founder of the Body Shop chain, developed her idea from the 'I could do that, but better' concept.

The first chapters in this section deal with generating your own ideas and the later chapters are concerned with how you can benefit from other people's ideas. The last chapter gives you some ideas of how to create a preliminary sieve through which you can put your ideas: an important exercise to avoid wasting time evaluating an opportunity that could have been easily eliminated earlier.

Chapter Six:
Recognizing Needs

Introduction

All people and organizations have needs which they fulfil in many different ways. When you can fulfil those needs better than they are currently being met, then you will almost certainly have a business opportunity. As this book illustrates, there are essentially two ways you can generate a business idea. They stem from the following attitudes:

- 'I can do this (say, welding) therefore I will set up a business selling it'
- 'What do people want and is there any way I can provide it?'

As approaches, they can both result in solid businesses, but I would be happier investing in the second because that approach solves a problem from the customers' point of view rather than a supplier's. When trying to develop ideas from the demand side you will need to increase your awareness of:

- your own environment
- other people's and organizations' needs
- the distinction between benefits and features

The Employer as Customer

Many people set up firms to service an employer's needs. Wherever you may be working it is you who can see, far more clearly than anyone else, what it is your employer needs – perhaps in terms of quality improvements in the base products, or perhaps in terms of improved delivery dates, or even after-sales services. There are all sorts of things that you might be able to do better (from your employer's point of view) than the existing suppliers. For example, take Bob Corwin:

Bob is an ex-IBM salesman. When selling he always felt that he did not have enough information on his prospective customers to make the most efficient use of his time. For example, it would have been useful to know in advance what machines they used and how old the machines were – if the machines were newish, the likelihood of a sale was much reduced. Bob now runs a company providing very specialized market research, including the above and much more. His first client was IBM.

Admittedly, Bob did not set up his business just to service IBM, and indeed he now has some other excellent quality clients. But he did first spot the need in IBM and always intended that the first contracts would be with them because he already knew how to sell and to whom in the company – it assured him of a good start.

In fact, this is one of the major advantages of setting up a business in response to an identified need in your employer. Many businesses that have other companies as their customers have difficulty identifying their actual customer by name. People often make the mistake of assuming that because it is a purchasing department's signature on a purchase order, the requirement for the goods originated there. For a successful sale in other words, all you have to do is persuade the purchasing manager that you are the bee's knees and all will be well. Not so, I am afraid – the purchasing department normally responds to needs elsewhere in the organization, rather than originating them themselves.

The Buying Manager may have control over which supplier to use, but not the influence to raise the orders in the first place. One has to find out who influences or makes the decisions to purchase and sell in part, or in whole. You already know your way around the firm and if you are not already acquainted with the people you will be selling to, you will certainly know someone who can introduce you. You will have the competitive advantage over other suppliers simply because of your better knowledge of the customer.

How do you take advantage of this? The answer involves you in changing the way you look at your workplace and its environment, asking yourself the following questions:

- Are the purchasing people bemoaning the fact that they are having difficulties of any sort? Could I help them overcome a problem?
- Is there anything I can do to help the sales force to become more effective?
- Are my colleagues complaining about not being able to do their work for any reason? Can I help overcome that problem?
- Analyze the factory and production stoppages over the last year or two.

Is there a product or service that I might supply that would have helped to keep the factory going?
- What would make me and my colleagues work more effectively? Can I supply it?
- What would make my colleagues my own and working environment better (thus leading to greater motivation and hence, the theory goes, productivity)? Can I supply it?
- Could the job I am doing be sub-contracted for my current firm or to any other?

If you spend some time you could probably add many more ways of looking at your environment to this list. Listen especially to people who are complaining: while they may be irritating you in some respects you should understand that they are also pointing out to you a deficiency which may represent an opportunity to you.

> David Soul listened to the coach drivers his firm employed. They always complained that the brushes available for cleaning the outsides of their coaches were no good. He designed and launched a brush and portable cleaning system for coach and lorry drivers who do not have access to automatic cleaners.

Be very careful that you do not lose your job in the process of searching for ideas. If you demonstrate to others that you are thinking of going it alone *before* you are actually ready to do so, your employer will soon assess your divided loyalties; often loyalties which actually conflict with the best interests of your employer. When you are ready, your best bet is to approach the person who will gain from your improvement (the factory manager, the sales manager, etc.) and persuade him or her that:

- the change is worth considering
- you are the person to provide whatever it is you think needs providing.

If successful, you'll then have someone who is actively backing your suggestion *before* you make any official approaches. If you are unsuccessful in your presentation, the fact that only one person knows of your intentions will serve as a sort of 'damage-limitation' exercise. You should perhaps invest in some chain-mail armour to protect your back from the many knives which will surely come thudding in your direction!

The Employer as an Idea Generator

Not only can your employer be an excellent source of ideas for businesses set up specifically to sell back into the old company, but they can also be a major, and some say the best, source of ideas for businesses selling to other people. In these cases, the ideas are generated by looking at the employer's activities to see if there is anything they are missing or not doing quite as well as you might. Such new business ideas tend to come from three categories:

- a duplication of what the employer is currently doing;
- a new market that the employer has not exploited
- generating a new product idea while working for the employer.

Business ideas that are generated through your own employer are considered to be the best as you will use the knowledge, experience and skills that you've gained working for the firm. Consequently, you need not scratch around in an attempt to gain the abilities and skills necessary to fulfil the claims you make for your products or services.

> Frank Meyer worked in the optical robots division of a large technical university. He started his own business using similar technology to that of his employer.

This implies, by the way, that if you do not have experience in the business you plan to start, it would benefit tremendously if you were to work for an outlet similar to the one you plan to open. From my own experience, for example, I caution those of you who want to open vegetarian restaurants: please go and work for one or two. Those of you who remain firmly committed after such experience (the very few) will be in the enviable position of starting from the strength of experience. Far too many people want to start vegetarian restaurants without *any* knowledge of catering at all, let alone vegetarianism.

Duplication

Duplication of what the employer is doing is very common in new starts. You simply take the experience, knowledge and skills that you have developed over the years and start applying it for yourself rather than for your employer.

> Alan Goodman used to work for a large technological consultancy called PA Technology. When he joined

them he already had a degree in a related field, and
during the ten years or so that he worked for the firm he
built on that. Two years ago, he and some like-minded
(and like-experienced) people set up their own technological consultancy and came to Cranfield to get help
in the early development of the business.

This method of entrepreneurial venture is not quite as simple as it sounds.
You will be trying to establish a business in a marketplace that has proven,
and possibly successful, competition: your own employer, at the very least. If
you do go this route, you must be able to offer something over and above
what your employer currently provides. You must be able to do it better in
some ways: what I would call 'strategy improvements'. These improvements
can come from a fairly wide variety of factors, including:

- more focused marketing
- inexpensiveness
- new materials
- shorter lead times for the customer
- better after-sales service
- higher quality: better value for money

If you cannot do all of this and more, there is absolutely no reason why the
customer should change from his or her established supplier, (your employer) with whom they have built up a track record and whose virtues and
faults they already know, to a supplier with no proven abilities on the
marketplace (you) and who is an unknown quantity.

New market

New markets that your employer has not exploited can often come to light.
Companies can, and do, move on in their commercial focus, sometimes
leaving whole markets behind. Often, entire markets can be ignored: those
that might simply be too small for them to consider worth exploiting, but
which for you, especially at the early stages of production, could be extremely
profitable. This potential area is considered in much more depth in Chapter
13.

Generating a new product idea

Generating a new product idea while working for your employer is also fairly
common. For example, take Edward Carr:

Edward worked on the technological side of a large computer manufacturer and came up with an idea for speech synthesis, using computers. This was a side development from the work he had been doing. He left the company to be able to exploit it, and persuaded his old university to let him use some of their equipment to build a bench prototype, which is as far as it has gone up to date. It holds great promise.

You do have to be careful, however, that you are not taking specialist knowledge that your employer holds rights to.

The Complaints Department

I mentioned earlier that you should listen carefully to people at work who complain. Very often complaints are derived from legitimate circumstances that can represent exploitable opportunities to you. This is true of your environment as a whole – personal and work. When anyone finds the need to complain, they are really saying that whatever event has caused this complaint has not lived up to their expectations. They had a 'need', identified through their perception of what should have happened, which was not in actuality satisfied.

Stephanie Clairedale lived close to a Chinese takeaway in London. She had eaten the food on a number of occasions but didn't think much of it; neither did most of the other people in the area, as she discovered when she started listening to their complaints. She decided that she could do better herself and set up five doors away. She now has a thriving trade in Chinese takeaway food.

To spot opportunities listen to complaints; when they arise do not dismiss them, but get the complainants to expand on what it was they were expecting, and how the goods or service failed to fulfil them. Examine the cause of the discrepancy to see if there is anything you can do to alleviate it. Don't worry at this stage about the number of people complaining – one is enough. The numbers' game comes later when you are checking to see if there are enough people with the same needs to support any business you might subsequently set up (*see Part III*).

What Do People Want?

If you can come up with an understanding of what people need then you will probably be able to create a sound business. It is not necessarily as difficult as it sounds – the recognition of complaints is one method of identifying peoples' unfulfilled needs and wants. Nor is it necessarily the invention of new technological wonders, although some of these needs are obvious and thus easy to spot, such as voice recognition computers, in the drive to get round the drawbacks of communicating through a keyboard (as I am doing right now).

People want reliable builders and decorators, or so they say. In fact, it is perfectly possible that people want builders to be entirely as unreliable as they are now just so that they can continue to carp about the troubles they had. Trying to work out what peoples' needs and wants are requires in you a frame of mind based on the question: 'how can I improve this person's life?'

Trends

Spotting trends can help in identifying peoples' needs. For example, the growth of the home computer markets has spawned a large number of ancillary related businesses, including:

- – many specialist magazines
- – a second-hand dealer network
- – many software houses
- – specialist suppliers

There are dozens more.

If you can spot a real trend as it starts to take off, you will also spot many opportunities to profit from helping people make more use of whatever the trend is. Such as Malcolm Turff, an ex-RAF electronics specialist, who took advantage of a growing trend when he started his business installing satellite TVs. I used the words 'real trend' to distinguish this from fashions and fads. One can make long lasting and very profitable businesses from fashions and fads but they are inherently risky. With trends you are looking for permanent changes in the way people do things and changes in society as a whole. This will give any businesses that can take advantage of a trend a solid demand for their product.

How do you spot trends? It is not always easy. One way of doing it is to take an area of society, work, leisure, tourism or family with which you are very familiar, and work out what has changed in this area between now and this time last year. Or this time three years ago. Ask yourself if the changes appear permanent, and if so you have probably isolated a trend. There is now a publication which can help you to spot trends. It is called 'Trend Monitor' and is published by Aslib/TMI at Aspen House, 14 Station Road, Kettering, Northants, NN15 7HE; telephone (0536) 513501.

Market Gaps

Markets for products and services are not perfect in the way that they satisfy their customers' needs: 'gaps' can, therefore, exist where the existing sources of supply are deficient in some way. For example:

> Fast food outlets sell not food, but convenience. One factor common to them all is the fact that you have to go to them to pick up the food – an inconvenience. This could be seen as a market gap, and indeed, a firm has just started to fill it. The company, Rickshaw, delivers meals to your home: every so often a menu falls through my letter box showing the range of foods, the prices and the times of day that they have set up delivery systems. If you want an evening meal it can be delivered at 6, 7, 8 or 9 o'clock. The first time I used them, I did so simply to see if they used a Rickshaw to deliver. They did not!

Identifying such gaps simply requires the same attitude of mind as in earlier examples, combined with keeping your eyes and ears open.

Conclusion

That last sentence leads me neatly to the conclusion of this chapter in that recognizing other people's needs and wants depends on:

- your mental attitude. You have to make yourself sympathetic to what others find important in life;
- keeping your eyes open. Because if you do not you will be blind to potential opportunities.

Chapter Seven:
Thinking for Opportunities

Introduction

According to Edison, invention is 99 per cent perspiration and 1 per cent inspiration.

It has been said that fortune favours the prepared mind. It is also possible that true creativity arises out of the mastery of your chosen path. You need look at the inspired performances of, say, ballet dancers to see that there is some truth in this. That is all right if you like ballet, which I do not, but it is also true of many disciplines. The craftsman, so dedicated to the techniques and skills required by his craft will produce a work of beauty. This sort of creativity is also needed in producing good business ideas.

This section will help you prepare your mind and produce mechanisms and techniques which put your thinking on the right track.

There are a number of ways of conceptualising the creative process. For example:

- creative, as opposed to analytical thinking, which is a relatively self-explanatory concept;
- divergent, as opposed to convergent thinking. Convergent is when your thoughts focus in on an area, as in problem solving, whereas divergent is where you start out from somewhere in your thoughts with no real idea of where you are going; and
- lateral, as opposed to vertical thinking.

However you conceptualize the process, you are going to have to become reasonably 'creative' if you are to end up with a potential winner in business terms. First, look at creativity itself.

Creativity

It has been suggested that the two halves of our brains have different functions[1]. The left side is said to influence or control: logic, reasoning, language, numeracy, analysis, linearity, the digital, the abstract.

1 Edwards B., *Drawing on the Right Side of The Brain*. Souvenir Press, 1981.

The right, however, is deemed to control: rhythm, music, imagination, images, colour, shape recognition, day dreaming, creativity.

If this is true, and the available research does back it up, then to be creative we need to use the right side of our brains, perhaps more than we have been doing recently. As an accountant of twenty years standing, I must be heavily left dominated. Actually, it is society which condemns us in this fashion, as you would know if you have seen the spark of interest wane when accountancy is mentioned at parties! Anyone can be creative – you should see some of my accountant friends' creative approach to the preparation of the company accounts on which you, your stockbroker, insurance company and pension funds rely when making investment decisions.

The point is, therefore, that you can improve on your existing level of creativity. To do this you have to do creative things and exercise the creative 'muscles' of your brain. For example, why not pick up a pen and any old scrap of paper and try to sketch whatever is currently in front of you. It does not matter how well or badly your efforts reflect the real thing, it matters only that you do it.

Practise being creative – it will make you more creative in all areas, including that of generating business ideas.

Barriers to creativity

There are several barriers to creativity, which, if they were not to exist in you, would make you far more creative than you currently are. Removing these barriers is essential to the production of useful business ideas.

Self-imposed barriers

We can impose barriers to creativity on ourselves. These can come in many forms, consciously or unconsciously, but perhaps the most common ailment is negativity. We tend to be negative in our approach to the 'new' – possibly an aspect of our larger fear of the unknown – even when it is our own brain that has developed the idea.

How do you change your attitude and become more positive in your response to new thoughts and ideas? The best way is to try to focus on the worthwhile part of any idea before dismissing it, no matter how stupid it might first appear. That way you will improve your ability to benefit from the ideas you create for yourself. Mentally pat yourself on the head each time you generate any idea or new thought at all.

Do not think of yourself as unimaginative – think of yourself instead as creative person. As a business trainer I often get people in accountancy sessions claiming that they never have been 'good at figures' and hence will be unable to understand. This is a classic example of a self imposed constraint.

My heart sinks when I hear it because, with that attitude, the person concerned will never take on board what is being said, no matter how easy. The thing which annoys me most, however, is that it is never true. All of us must have a fundamental understanding of even very advanced applied mathematics simply to get through each day, let alone the simple addition and ordering of numbers that accountancy involves.

For example, take the situation where two people are throwing a ball to each other on the beach. Each person catches it, usually with little or no problem. If you told them that the ball's flight itself was a result of a mixture of the force and direction with which it was thrown, the action of gravity, the air friction, the effect of air turbulence, and the rate and direction of the ball's spin, they would hesitate when next they caught it. If you also told them that to have their hand in a position to catch it, their minds must combine all these factors and manipulate them very quickly using differential calculus, amongst other techniques, then they would almost certainly drop it.

I do not believe that anyone is not 'good at figures'. Neither do I believe that anyone is unimaginative.

Patterns

If you are analytical in your thinking, it is natural to look for patterns or take the line that 'this is the only answer'. When you spot a pattern, any subsequent idea or thoughts have to be channelled into the pattern or they become convergent with it.

Conformity and fear of looking foolish

We all want to conform – the pressure exerted on us by our peer groups, friends or family, can be tremendous. Remember you are here to generate ideas rather than creating an image. What may appear stupid on the surface often has surprisingly commercial opportunities.

Not challenging the obvious

It is far too easy to accept the obvious. As you will see in a later section of this chapter, challenging the obvious can be a remarkably good source of ideas. Even if an answer exists (the obvious) we should look behind it to get at other, better ones.

Evaluating too quickly

We do this in our heads as the ideas crop up. We say things such as 'it is too silly' or 'this is not for me'. As a result we miss many ideas which could be refined into something worthwhile. Here again, it is necessary to tell ourselves to stop and to look at the good points of an idea before rejecting it.

I suggest that you concentrate on routes to achieving the objectives that you have, by now, set for yourself. This approach to ideas should make you consider questions such as, 'Will this further my goals?'. In any case, if you are anything like me, your perceptions of what your friends' perceptions of you actually are, will be totally wrong, and my family already thinks I am a fool!

Opportunity Search

> An opportunity is as real an ingredient in business as raw material, labour or finance – but it only exists when you can see it.[1]

This is how Edward deBono starts his excellent book on how to search for business opportunities and it is well worth looking at some of his ideas here. Although the book is written from the big company point of view, you might benefit from reading the original. As far as we are concerned, he has two areas which can be of major benefit. They are a starting out checklist and an end point checklist.

The starting out checklist gives a point of reference from which to begin a search, whereas the end point checklist gives a set of points at which to aim. The first is likely to get you to look at ideas which you might not otherwise have considered. The second focuses your thoughts on where you want to be. They are both worthwhile and are echoed by me in various different ways throughout this book. As I cover many of the same areas in other parts of this book, this is a brief summary.

Start point checklist

When using the start point checklist to generate ideas, you may end up with opportunities which initially look as though they are right outside your

---

1 deBono E., *Opportunities: A Handbook of Business Opportunities Search*, Pelican, 1980.

framework. You need not necessarily discard them – it would be better if you attempt to bring them within the framework by redefining them in some way.

Intrinsic assets

Intrinsic assets are those which are currently available to you. Ask yourself, your friends or family, 'What can I do with this?' and 'Are there any other uses?' The assets might include cash, your home, your car, or anything else you have to hand.

> A doctor friend of mine, has a large, secluded house on the outskirts of London. His garden contains an open-air swimming-pool, long unused by his family. He asked himself, 'What can I do with this?'. One idea was to rent it out to someone else. Refining the idea further, he asked 'Who would be interested in using this secluded but very attractive pool?' One of the suggestions was photographers in need of an outside location. His biggest customers are page three photographers from the *Sun*.

Operating assets

The way you currently run your life may result in the existence of some operating assets which could be put to other uses. For example, you may be sub-contracting in the building industry. If you are, there may well be up-front payments which you currently bank for subsistence during the life of the contract. Is there another way of using this money? Remember that, at the beginning there will be large surpluses. Could you use these more profitably?

If you always go the same way to work and back, at the same time each day, you have an operating asset which could be utilized, perhaps for a delivery service targeted at the firms along the route.

The way others do things might create an operating asset for you:

> John Wright had worked in the builders trade for years. He started a business called 'Stop-Gap' to take advantage of the fact that most suppliers in that industry have

minimum order sizes way in excess of what the smaller operator needs. He takes the large order in and sells it on in smaller quantities.

Situation assets

These arise from the environment in which we live. Most commonly they grow out of change in that environment. For example, the introduction of tax relief on investments in new companies (the Business Expansion Scheme) gave rise to a whole new breed of venture capital companies.

The change does not have to be on that scale:

> Tom Mason, who lives in Tunbridge Wells borrowed his father's chain saw and ladders in October 1987 and made a mint out of the situation assets that existed after that month's phenomenal gales.

Left behind

As companies grow and develop they leave behind markets which could provide opportunities. The move of many shops and stores into big sheds on the outskirts of town does not conveniently satisfy small, but important requirements of some customers. Would you drive all the way out to one of these stores, walking two miles across their car park and back again, just for the tin of baby milk that you did not realize you were low on?

Try to identify the most successful companies in your area over the last five years. Have they left a space behind during their recent growth?

Variable value

The value of anything is subjective to the user of that thing. Thus it is possible to make a business out of buying goods in from someone who has a relatively low value of them and taking them to sell to someone else who values them more. In the antique trade, 'runners' do precisely this. They buy from wherever they feel they can get a cheap price and, more often than not, sell on through one of the auction houses.

Antiques are not the only area where it works:

> Nick Beswick came to Cranfield for help in developing a business based on buying clothes from jumble sales and the like, cleaning and repackaging them for sale from stalls set up in student unions in colleges.

A very fashionable store – Flip – in Covent Garden only sells second hand American clothing.

Tabitha Severn bought 500 second hand silk kimonos (at 50p per kilo) on a recent trip to Japan. Like Nick, she cleans and repackages them before selling them on at tremendous profit.

Challenge

There are several reasons why things are done as they are, but this does not mean they always must be done that way. This sounds very vague. It is. You can apply this technique to anything at all. Take your workplace and choose the thing your company does best. Examine it to see if there are other, better ways of providing it or improving on it. If it's already successful this could be your way of creating a winner. You can do the same with something you value in your home.

De-averaging

Here you take a segment of the market place and try to segment it further. For example, your employer may be a manufacturer of cosmetics selling primarily to women under 25 years old. For your employer, this might be sufficient segmentation, but you could find within that group there are all sorts of people with differing needs. Perhaps the profession of the individual has an effect on their cosmetic purchases – secretaries may buy more lipsticks than check-out attendants – and you may be able to satisfy their requirements better than is currently being done.

In fact, one company, Isis, has just been formed to manufacture a range of products specifically for groups of people whose ethnic origin and hence skin tones are outside of that catered for by the existing manufacturers.

Transfer

This involves taking a process with which you are familiar and seeing if it could be applied to any other areas. Say that you work in a bakery. There will be all sorts of different processes going on at any one time. Will any of these help make other business areas more effective? Perhaps one could apply the same techniques to spray finishing.

End point checklist

Whereas the start point checklist begins from the place you are now the end point checklist has as its premise the question, 'Where do we want to be?' Essentially, you look at what the ending position might be, and look for ideas which could get you there. The end point checklist is as follows.

The 'something' method

Using this method involves defining the characteristics of the end product or service and then trying to establish what fits in with them.

> Michael Roberts decided that he wanted to run his own business after he left college. He unwittingly used the 'something' method to develop his ideas. The criteria he developed for a new product, not knowing what the product itself would be, were that it should:
>
> - be sufficiently different in its features and benefits in order to stop it being price sensitive – thus it would have the ability to achieve a high price;
> - little or no advertising costs necessary for the launch, or
> - the subsequent operation;
> - functional features should be built in;
> - require short production lead times;
> - have the ability to take an existing design and alter it so as to achieve the shortest design lead time possible;
> - the ability to have large ranges of models;
> - be capable of achieving large volumes of sales;
> - be easy to manufacture;
> - open up new markets;
> - be of perceived quality;
> - the sales features should be apparent;
> - be of aesthetic appearance; and
> - aimed at a definite market.
>
> (Michael eventually came to Cranfield seeking help to launch a business marketing a range of stereo headphones/sunglasses called Sonic Specs.)

Quality improvements

This is another method in which you take other peoples' products or services as the basis for your own business. I cover this methodology in the next chapter.

Defects and faults

Here you can take the products or services of another organization and ask:

- what does this product lack? (defects)
- what defects does this product have?
- what faults would we like to do away with?

This allows you to improve on other peoples products and services. (*See chapter 8.*)

Visualization

This technique is more normally associated with art and other 'creative' areas.[1]. However, if you have watched some of the deals and new businesses sprout and grow over the years, you would realize that 'creativity' is not the sole preserve of the artist and his or her ilk. Visualization has been used for centuries, but for some reason is unpopular with psychologists, and hence we hear little of it. It can and has been used in getting businesses off the ground. In fact, Conrad Hilton, of Hilton Hotel fame, called the first chapter of his autobiography 'You've Got To Dream'[2].

You need to create visual pictures of:

- customers;
- products/services;
- places;
- financing the deal;
- what business you want to be in;
- levels of service; and
- layout (especially where the vision is of a restaurant or other business where the surroundings are one of the more important factors).

1 Rockey E. H., *Envisioning New Business: How Entrepreneurs Perceive The Benefits of Visualisation*, Frontiers of Entrepreneurship Research, 1986, Babson College, Mass., USA.
2 Hilton C., *Be My Guest*, Prentice Hall Inc., 1957.

Lie on a beach, sit in a darkened room – anything to get your mind working on a picture of your own future. It really does not matter how or where you develop the pictures, only that you do. Use deep breathing and other relaxation techniques to get yourself in the right frame of mind.

As a process, it can help in all the fundamentally important areas of developing a business idea to the stage where you are willing to devote some time to checking out its feasibility. The major areas are:

- – personal goal setting;
- – idea generation;
- – idea evaluation;
- – developing a strategy for each worthwhile idea in turn; and
- – strategy evaluation (the checking out of an idea for its feasibility).

In the area of personal goals:

> Ernest Obeng is one of this country's fastest runners over 100 metres. On one occasion he said:
> 'To be able to win you must visualize yourself breaking the tape. The major problem is that all the other participants have the same dream.' He now applies the same techniques to his sports consultancy business, which he founded in 1987.

The process of developing a picture in your mind automatically helps with generating ideas about what sort of business you should start. Try on the pictures like hats. Do they fit you? Are you happy with them? Do you like the image they create?

It also automatically helps with idea evaluation, in that any pictures with which you feel uncomfortable can be discarded at this stage.

Directed dreaming and visualizing is probably the first step anyone should take in strategic planning. Try to pre-view the entire enterprise. It helps to answer the three major strategy questions:

- – where are we going?
- – when will we get there?
- – how will we know that we have arrived?

You need not worry about clarity or getting the full picture right first time. If you do it several times over, clarity will come. Write it down afterwards and talk to somebody about it – share the vision to get refinements. It is a tremendous confidence builder – you have sorted out many of the problems which might have occurred before they arise.

Brainstorming

As a technique, everyone has heard of brainstorming, and because everyone has heard of it, without knowing too much about it, it is much misused. Most people who try this simply get together as a group without preparation or planning, with no clear idea of what to do or how to guide the event, and then wonder why it has not solved their life's problems.

Essentially, brainstorming is a means of getting a large number of ideas from a group of people in a short time. Here we are talking of a minimum of five people and a maximum of ten – they need to feed off one another but not swamp anyone in the session – and between one and three hours. It does not matter how good or bad the ideas are because you are interested in quantity not quality.

Guidelines

Suspend judgement

Having taken all the time and trouble to build the framework suggested by Part I of this book – you must temporarily set it aside. Do not use it in the brainstorming session because it is a form of judgement and evaluation. As you saw from an earlier section of this chapter, evaluation and judgement will inhibit innovation. At all costs, try to avoid saying things such as; that is not for me, that is too stupid, or what sort of fool do you take me for, and other negative statements during a brainstorming session. If you cannot restrain yourself you will be doing yourself out of some very interesting ideas because the group members will start using your evaluations of the ideas that occur to them before they mention them publicly. Judging ideas as they are produced restricts creativity in a big way.

Freewheel

Try to get the group's participants to roam widely whilst the session is running. There is a suggestion later about how to do this. (See page 94)

Quantity

It is worth repeating that quality in the ideas produced in a brainstorming session is irrelevant. The more ideas that are produced, the better off you will be in terms of usable ideas later.

Cross fertilize

You actively want the group members' ideas to spark off other ideas, either in their own minds or in someone else's.

Stages of brainstorming

It has been suggested that you should follow a laid out structure.[1] This excellent format is as follows:

State the problem and discuss

Give the group sufficient information to let them see problems, but not enough to allow them to become analytical. Some of the group will already be familiar with the problem and this can represent a difficulty as their thinking will already be analytical. Try to avoid detail in terms of background.

Restate the problem

Here, let the others in the group put forward their own ideas of what the problem is – let them restate it, writing down each restatement. By restating the problem you get to see some of the other aspects involved in the problem. You should be aiming to get at least 20 restatements. It may surprise you that there are so many different ways of looking at the problem – some of which could be of great value subsequently.

In writing, use felt tip on large sheets of paper. You can then put the completed sheets on the wall for inspection which will allow cross fertilization.

Warm up session

Here, you try to generate the freewheeling atmosphere that brainstorming depends on. You get the group to suggest 'other uses for . . .'. Try it with something lighthearted and try to get silly responses as well as serious ones. You do not need to write anything down.

---

1   Rawlinson J. G., *Creative Thinking and Brainstorming*, Wildwood House Ltd., 1986.

Select a basic restatement

Select a basic restatement and write it down, starting with the words 'In how many ways can we. . . ?' Use it to head up a new sheet of paper (it will save people forgetting which restatement is being worked on).

Brainstorm

Read out the restatement and call for ideas. Hopefully, if you have got the atmosphere and other factors right, the flow of ideas should be quite fast. Write them down as they appear, summarising in the process. If you get the summarizing wrong it will not matter – in fact it may be beneficial as the person whose idea it was will tell you that they did not mean what you wrote but some other thing and then you have two ideas. Number the ideas and as you fill each sheet put it up on the wall for the group members to look at. This helps cross fertilization. If you use a flip chart do not just 'flip', use it to reassess at intervals.

Encourage laughter and noise, since that seems to have a beneficial effect on the flow of ideas. Repeat the ideas as they are spoken and encourage more by saying 'yes' from time to time. Laugh with (not at) the wild ideas. If the flow stutters, stop for a minute's silence to let the participants think.

Eventually the flow will dry up. Take another restatement and see if you can get it going again with that. Use as many of the restatements, sequentially, as possible in this way.

Wildest idea

To wind up the session take the wildest idea and ask the group to see if it can come up with ideas which will allow the wild one to be made sensible. You may even get some excellent ideas out of this final stage.

Evaluation

It is best to wait a day or two before beginning the evaluation. Let things settle in your mind and then use the techniques laid out in Chapter 13.

Morphological analysis

This is an idea generator with tremendous potential. At its simplest, one prepares a grid with a number of elements on each axis. For example, suppose you are experienced in the cosmetics industry and have decided that you want to use that experience in starting your own business, you can use Morphological Analysis in the search for new products to market for yourself.

IDEA GRID

Age Sold To

	under 18	18 to 25	26 to 35	36 to 50	51 to 65	over 65
Mascara						
Foundation cream						
Lipsticks						
Eye shadow						
Fragrances						
Hair products						
Nail products						
Skin products						

Possible Products

You now have a grid containing 48 ideas. The first box on the first line would be to sell mascara to under eighteen-year-olds. The first box on the second line suggests that you sell foundation creams to the same group. The last box on the last line has the idea that you market skin products to the over sixty-five age-group. You might feel that these ideas are insufficient on their own and need further refining. You might feel that you would need to consider, say, the customer's profession, thus:

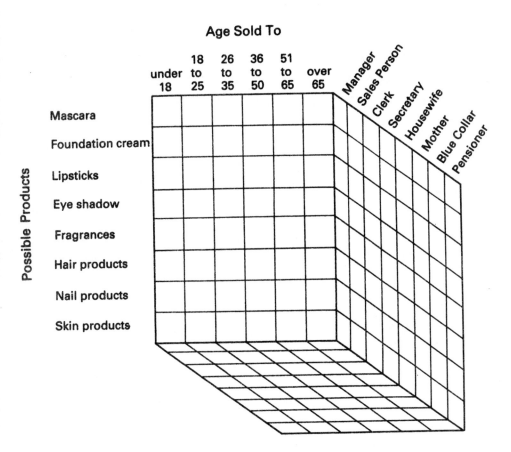

You now have a box containing 336 ideas (8 × 6 × 7). The largest number of these ideas will be useless to you. For example, one of the ideas in the box would have you marketing mascaras to managers under eighteen years old. It is not impossible, but there would probably be too few sales to be worth bothering with. At this stage you are concerned with generating large numbers of ideas, not with their quality. That comes later. You are trying to get to the few feasible ideas but without generating large numbers of ideas first, the number of attractive ideas you end up with will be not just few, but very few.

You can extend the number of ideas by adding a fourth axis (taking us into four dimensional mathematics, were we to try to draw it). Suppose you feel that the nationality or ethnic background of the customer was important, your fourth dimension could be European, Afro-Caribbean, Asian, Chinese, Other.

Here you would have a grid with 1,680 ideas ($8 \times 6 \times 7 \times 5$). You will probably need a computer to work out and list every permutation and combination.

Add a fifth dimension. Perhaps the gender of the customer affects things: by adding the male/female dimension you double up to 3,360 ideas. Perhaps it is a good thing that there are only two sexes, because you can see that as more dimensions are added it can get very unwieldy.

This idea generation technique, like brainstorming, can be used with groups of people who would help you develop the dimensions and the elements within each dimension.

Where you do generate more than three dimensions, you will have a problem in evaluating them because of the numbers of ideas which are generated. To handle this you could start with the first three dimensions, evaluating as you are going along. Here, the objective is to cut the first three dimensions down to two (or even one) before going on to add the fourth dimension. If you do this it allows the use of diagrammatical presentation (the grid and box) for all dimensions and this makes it easier for this participants in the process to conceptualize additional dimensions and elements, enhancing their creativity.

Conclusion

However you create ideas, you need some mechanism for sorting the ideas which are useless to you from those which are worth spending some more time on. Chapter 13 deals with ways you can sort the wheat from the chaff.

This chapter has dealt mainly with ways in which you can generate ideas for yourself or enhance your own creativity. The remainder of this section of the book goes on to deal with the situations through which you can benefit from someone else's idea.

Chapter Eight:
Specific Routes to Ideas

Introduction

It is perfectly possible that such idea generation processes outlined in the last Chapter could still leave you without an idea with which you feel comfortable. In this event, do not despair because there are traditional specific routes to ideas which you can explore to try to find an attractive opportunity. This chapter deals with the traditional routes, including such areas of search as:

- how to improve on services offered by existing businesses;
- transferring businesses from one location to another;
- selling other peoples' products;
- turning hobbies into businesses;
- licensing;
- inventions;
- published sources of ideas; and
- other organizations which can help.

Improving on existing businesses

This is one of the classical ways of getting into business for yourself. What you do is to look at other businesses and ask yourself two questions:

- 'Could I do that?', and
- 'Can I do it *better?*'.

If the answer to both questions is yes, then you have an opportunity on your hands. You not only have just an opportunity, but an excellent opportunity.

> Jennie Smith had lots of experience as a secretary. She saw that her local Enterprise Agency was offering 'nursery' units for the small businesses of her town, Luton. (Nursery units are small areas or offices in

99

larger buildings where firms can move in and out easily on monthly rentals. They usually have some sort of shared facilities too, a telephonist, telex, fax, etc.)

Jennie saw that these units were going like hot cakes – the Enterprise Agency had proved that a market existed. She felt that she too could provide such units, along with the advantages of shared facilities. Hers would be 'better' because she would get more up-market premises, provide wider services, including secretarial and reception facilities, and let small, but quality, offices.

Her thriving business, called Trend House Business Centre, helped her to win Luton's Businesswoman of the Year Award.

The 'me too' approach to starting your own firm has some big advantages. It lets other people test the demand for you. All you need do is just copy what is currently being done, improving on the way it is being done, if you can. The originators of the business may have overcome awareness problems for you, such as the obstruction to sales caused by no-one knowing that such products or services exist. And, since they have already made the mistakes, you ought to be in better position from a number of different viewpoints right from the beginning of your business; for example, you will already have a good idea of which promotional methods work best.

The biggest problem with this idea generation technique lies in the second question – what constitutes 'better'? Essentially, better means some sort of quality improvement, and quality in this context has a very wide interpretation.

Quality improvements

There are many ways in which a product can be improved. These might include, simplifying, bettering the customer appeal, improving cost effectiveness or reliability, creating greater production efficiency, increasing the quality, better marketing, and greater convenience.

Simplifying

There are all sorts of products which are complex to operate but which we continue to buy every day. The newest of these is the computer and already people are driving towards making it simpler to use.

The software I am using to write this book is an example. It was designed by three students Leo, Andy and Ian, whilst still at college. It is not a word processor, but a 'report outliner' and its major benefits to me are that it involves very little investment of time in learning how to use it when compared to becoming proficient with a word processing package (four hours against two weeks). Leo, Andy and Ian have now set up a business called Thought Support Systems to market the software which is called Clarity.

Customer appeal

Enhancing the appeal of a product to the customer could also lead to good opportunities. Many products reach the market place by taking an established product and adding new features.

There is a toy on the market at the moment called the Dragon Lock, developed by a Cranfield technician called Mark Williams. It consists of plastic base, some brightly coloured rings and a chromium plated metal slide, which comes interwoven with the rings. The objective of the puzzle is to remove the slide. Mark brought the toy to me when it was in its prototype stage and subsequently attended a Cranfield programme to help get the idea on to market in the most favourable way. This lead to the establishment of a company to exploit the opportunity called Tag Toys.

While we were helping in the early launch phase there was a scare that a competitor was considering launching a product with all Tag Toy's features and some more of its own – once the puzzle had been solved, the base could be unlocked using the slide and the child would then have his or her own secret box. I do not know why it was never pursued because it would undoubtedly have been a success after all our efforts to get the Dragon Lock on to market.

At a recent open evening at Cranfield, Mark, who deprecatingly refers to Tag Toys as that 'potty little outfit', laid the success of the Dragon Lock at Cranfield's door, and in particular, its Firmstart programme which helped him and Tag Toys into business.

If you can find a Dragon Lock or similar product to which you can add features, you will probably be able to find a ready market for it. The sellers of the original product have opened up the market place for you. They were the ones with awareness problems. You have a ready made customer list too – those people who currently stock the original product ought to buy yours because, if you have got the added benefits right, your product should be more attractive to their customers.

Cost effectiveness

If you can make a product cheaper to the buyer then you might also have a commercial idea. You may be able to manufacture it out of less expensive materials. Alternatively you may be able to have a cheaper delivery system.

This is a dangerous route through which to open a business in an established market place because it invites price wars from the existing players in the market. So your cost cutting has to be defensible – there has to be something about it which the competition cannot copy.

Cost effectiveness in this sense can also be produced by improving the manufacture in some way.

Production efficiency

If you can use less skilled labour or use labour more efficiently than the existing suppliers of a product do, as you can pass these over to the customer, making the product cheaper to buy. Are there now machines that will do the job faster?

> I mentioned John Douglas of Penforth Sofa Beds in chapter 2. In the manufacture of Chesterfields a large number of buttons have to be sewn in by hand. John has introduced a simple but effective mechanism which can semi-automate the sewing of the buttons and thus has saved himself half the labour cost of that job.

Reliability

Improving the reliability of a product or service can often be a winner.

> John's sofa beds, whilst being excellent value for money, are not too different from other middle market

sofa beds which you can buy. What is very different, is that he has short, and more importantly, reliable delivery times. If a salesperson in a shop has not got the model or colour that the customer requires in stock, he can be confident that his delivery date promise to that customer will be met.

Anyone who can set up a reliable building firm ought to make a mint.

Quality

Here the objective is to make the product more attractive through increasing its quality. It may be just in terms of looks or by using better materials. Try to keep any associated price increase lower than the perceived increase in 'value', and so gain better value for money in the eyes of the buyer.

Marketing

Many companies rely on the tried and tested when it comes to the marketing of their product. You may be able to improve on this and thus create a successful idea.

> When Chantal Coady started her chocolate shop on the King's Road in Chelsea, she did not place adverts in the local papers or anything of that nature, but encouraged the press to write about her. She even managed to get into the Sunday Times magazine: a photograph showing her full length, propped against silk cushions, being quoted as proselytising chocolates as an aphrodisiac. She continues to create human interest stories for the press to pick up.

Convenience

People are willing to pay large sums for anything which is more convenient than their existing source of supply.

One writer[1] has given an extremely valuable technique for discovering of a product or service its capabilities for improvement. It involves asking oneself three questions:

---

1 Gray D. A., *The Entrepreneur's Complete Self-Assessment Guide*, Kogan Page, 1987.

- How can I make it. . . ?
- How can I improve. . . ?, and
- How can I. . . ?

How can I make it. . . ?

- safer,
- cleaner,
- slower,
- faster,
- at home (saving overheads),
- more convenient,
- less expensive.
- more pleasant,
- automatic,
- easier to package, store, transport,
- self-contained, portable, mobile, or disposable,
- easier to use,
- less expensive to replace, repair, re-use,
- easier to clean, maintain, lubricate, or adjust,
- more attractive and appealing,
- lighter, stronger, adjustable, thinner, or foldable,
- quieter or louder,
- less dangerous,
- reversible,
- dual or multi-functional.

How can I improve . . . ?

- its availability or distribution,
- its production,
- its design,
- its marketing.

How can I . . . ?

- subcontract its manufacture,
- teach it more quickly,
- cut costs of material and labour,
- combine it with or add it on to other products or services,
- condense or enlarge its size,
- exert less effort, time, and energy when dealing with it,
- add new features,
- accessorize it,
- remove any irritating feature or side effect.

As you can see, there are lots of ways you can improve products and services, all of which have the major advantage that you will be entering a proven market.

New to a location

Another classic route to generating ideas involves transferring businesses from one geographical area to another.

> Hussein Shakir saw a fast photo development service operating in London, realized that it required few technical skills since the process was highly automated, and decided that his home town of Sheffield would support such an outlet if he could get the right town centre premises.

This idea generation process needs the identification of two factors:

- a business idea which you can both put into action and can transfer, and
- a geographical area in which to locate the business so that it stands a good chance of success.

In both cases it is a matter of keeping your eyes open and your brain alert to potential relocation opportunities. It also means that you must travel a certain amount – if you rarely leave your home town you will find it hard to spot any businesses which may be capable of transfer. And the easiest place in which to locate your new idea is usually your home town because that is the one you know best. You can more easily spot the right locations and latent need for the new product, service, or even process.

A common variation on this theme is to bring the idea in from abroad. When you go overseas, you often see businesses operating which could have a lot of potential at home.

> Another example, this time of a business associated with Cranfield, is that of 'Froghurt'. Froghurt is the trading name for Matt and Tessa Rosenblat's business. Whilst vacationing in California during a break from her studies at the London School of Economics, Tessa saw yoghurt being sold in the same way as ice cream often is in this country – soft, served from ice cream machines. She liked the taste and the fact that it was

healthier than ice cream. She and Matt decided that they would set up such a business and when they had finished their degrees, came on a course at Cranfield to explore the idea further.

After many slips twixt cup and lip, they have finally (August 1988) set up retailing their Froghurt from a unit in the Gateshead Metrocentre. Success has gone to their heads – they are already looking for outlet number two.

I suppose the moral of these tales is that travel not only broadens your horizons, it can change your life dramatically.

Turning hobbies into businesses

This, too, is a common route to generating business ideas. Examine your hobbies to see if they have any commercial applications:

Eileen Early had been a rabbit fancier (the name applied to keen rabbit hobbyists) for fifteen years before she came to Cranfield for help in commercializing her hobby. She had already started the commercialization process by buying a largish home with three acres in Croydon, near Royston in Cambridgeshire. She did not realize that many of the services she was supplying free had a commercial value.

From this property she now runs a rabbit zoo, with up to 600 rabbits at some times of the year. Both children and adults love to visit and a half day spent there is excellent value for money if you can resist the charms of buying a rabbit for yourself – her more exclusive breeds go for hundreds of pounds each.

If you do have a hobby at which you are reasonably expert, there is a good chance that you can create a useful business idea. There may also be a route to your own business through selling the things your other hobbyist colleagues need such as magazines, specialist supplies and so on.

Selling other peoples' products

If you can sell, you may be able to create a business idea based on that capability.

> Richard Farrar came to Cranfield after a fairly long stint in the Middle East. He is an experienced salesman. He is an Arabic speaker. He has wide experience and contacts in the Middle East. Naturally, he came up with the idea of helping British firms sell their products into the Arab countries, making a commission on the sales he brought to those firms.
>
> He now has a thriving business with a portfolio of clients whose major common characteristic is that their sales to the Arab countries are too small to justify having their own Middle Eastern representative.

If you know that you can sell other people's products and you do want to start this sort of business, you are left with just one problem: how to find the companies whose product you could sell.

There are two solutions to this problem, the first market oriented, and the second, product oriented.

Market

Look around the market places with which you are familiar to see if you can identify the sorts of products which are needed, and then find the suppliers of these products. Talk to your contacts, asking them if they are dissatisfied in any way with their existing sources of supply. This should point you at areas of opportunity.

Product

Using this approach you first find products that you think have good features and then try to identify the markets where these features are benefits.

There are two organizations which can help here; firstly, The British Agents Register[1], this organization matches agents and clients and has a monthly magazine called the *BAR Review* which has many adverts from

---

[1] British Agents Register, 24 Mount Parade, Harrogate, HG1 1BP.

companies needing agents; secondly, The Manufacturers' Agents Association[1], which also has a useful monthly magazine containing adverts from companies needing agents.

If you cannot identify the products this way, you will have to rely on your eyes and ears in finding products which may have value in the market places with which you are familiar.

Licensing

Similar to the concept of selling someone else's product is the idea of licensing some new technology, process or product from the owner of the knowledge. Here, what happens is that you start a business, probably both manufacturing and selling, based on someone else's invention. Often the licensor is an established business abroad who wants to get a foothold in the UK market, but prefers to let someone else (you) take the risks.

It differs from an agent's agreement in that, under licensing it is usually the licensee who manufactures the product, whereas an agent simply sells the goods without being involved in their manufacture.

> David Tucker, a sales manager for a firm manufacturing pressure valves, wanted to set up his own business. He knew that a West German company similar to his employer had recently launched a new product into their markets. He approached the German firm and came to an agreement that he should manufacture the new product under licence in the UK, and limit his sales efforts to this country and the US.

Many licensing deals start with the licensee being an agent and then switching to manufacture.

> Dudley Fisher owns a company called Adrec which started three years ago by selling catalytic heaters. These work through chemical reaction and are safer than most other forms of heating because there is no flame. He began selling these heaters under an arrangement where he bought them from the Spanish manufacturer but has now switched to making them himself under licence.

---

1 The Manufacturers' Agents Association, 13a West Street, Reigate, Surrey RH2 9BL.

Again the best way of spotting these opportunities is to travel abroad and keep your eyes and ears open. There are two sources of information which could help in your search. These are International Licencing Ltd,[1] who have a monthly magazine of same name, and Prestwick Publications[2] who produce periodicals such as *New from Europe*, *New from Japan*, and *New from the US*. These publications contain listings of advances in technology in the respective countries.

Inventions

'Invent a better mousetrap, and the world will beat a path to your door' is a truism which is not true.

Becoming an inventor is a tremendously arduous task. W. Friese-Greene in a letter to *The Times* published on 6 April 1904 describes the history of the invention of the Cinematograph:

> I have been working on this invention for over twenty years – that is to say, over ten years prior to the time that it was brought out commercially in 1894. In 1885, at a meeting of the Photographic Society, Pall Mall, I showed an apparatus for taking pictures by merely turning a handle. The camera was made for glass plates, but I specifically mentioned that it would be used for films in the future. At that time no suitable film was obtainable, although they were being experimented with. From that date until 1889 I continued experimenting and perfecting my invention, and in 1889 brought out my first patent for a camera for taking pictures on a celluloid film at the rate of 600 frames per minute. On 29th November 1893, I took out a further patent giving the improvements made up to that date, which patent not only covered the apparatus for taking the pictures, but also the apparatus for the projecting of the same upon a screen. This, in connexion with my patent of 1889, is the master patent on the cinematograph.

This example encapsulates the problems involved in inventing anything. Friese-Greene, who, in 1889, had the idea of synchronizing motion pictures

---

1 International Licencing Ltd, 92 Cannon Lane, Pinner, Mddx HA5 1HT tel 01 866 2812.
2 Prestwick Publications, P.O. Box 205, Burnt Hills, New York, NY12027.

with the phonograph, pre-dating talking picture by 40 years, died in 1921 – without a penny to his name.

Money *can* be made this way, though.

> Mark Sanders was interested in folding bikes whilst he was studying for his Master's Degree in Industrial Design at the Royal College of Art. His project for the degree became a new invention for folding bikes, based on a triangular frame and using plastic as much as possible, especially for the 'chain' (which is actually a belt).
>
> When he came to Cranfield for help in exploiting his invention, he wanted to both manufacture and sell the bike himself. It soon became clear that this was beyond his resources, and could lead to the situation where he, as a very small manufacturer of an excellent product, would have his technology and patents 'leapfrogged' by a larger competitor. This is the situation where a company recognizes a good product and invests money in developing the idea further, so far, in fact, that they end up with a new and patentable product.
>
> All this implied that he had to get himself some muscle in the market place, which in turn led him to licensing the product to a manufacturer (not of bikes) who had strong contacts in the US market.
>
> Mark gets a royalty on each of the bikes sold and was also able to arrange a consultancy with the licensee to help take the bike from prototype to manufacture.

It is a long and hard route to take. Mark's folding bike took two years to bring on to the market after the prototype stage, which was itself two years after invention. Most inventions never see the light of day.

Chapter Nine:
Buying a business

Introduction

The easiest route for anyone starting out in business is to buy someone else's business.

> Valerie Evans wanted to get into business for herself using her knowledge of art and artists. After much to-ing and fro-ing she bought an artists' material retail shop in Greenwich. In addition to the materials such as paints, the shop also provided a framing service and made good sales out of prints to the tourists who jam the streets of Greenwich during the summer. The previous owner was retiring and wanted to realize his major asset.

This route into business can be fraught with difficulties, it is true, but it does have some pretty strong points in its favour.

Advantages

One of the major advantages that buying a business has over setting up your own from scratch, is that it has already been established by someone else and ought to have less risk involved. I use the word, ought, because not all businesses which are for sale are necessarily sufficiently solid in their position within a market to allow me to say, is. When buying a going concern you have the chance to benefit from the knowledge, experience and skills which were used to get the business to where it is now – hence you need less of these things yourself.

An existing business has some things which an entirely new business does not. These include, amongst others:

- a proven market – the business has been trading and therefore there is proof that it has 'something' – people have been willing to part with hard earned cash in its direction.
- an existing labour force – where the business is bigger than just the owner and immediate family, there will be a labour force (although that description might over-dignify it) already in place.
- established suppliers – you do not have to immediately go out and find suppliers, there will be a list available to you. In addition, the suppliers are already aware of the business and how successfully (or otherwise) it trades and hence getting credit should be less of a problem.
- an amount of goodwill – a good track record with customers may have been built up by the owner which will, hopefully, pass to you. The business already has a name for itself.

Because it is a going concern, you are buying into an existing profits and cash flow stream. When you start your own business, you will very often find that it can take quite a long time before the firm becomes profitable. Until it does you have to find extra capital to cover your living expenses – with a business you have just bought you should be in a position to be able to take an income on which to live straight away and without needing to find extra funding.

There is far less pressure on you when buying a business and it is fast. You do not have to find premises, buy equipment separately, or recruit, find customers, or find suppliers.

It is also possible that the business that you buy has been underperforming in some way, it may have:

- underoptimization of sales from the existing customer base;
- very slow collection of money from customers;
- inefficient use of assets;
- inefficient use of labour;
- poor suppliers;

If you can turn these around, you can make the existing business more profitable from day one.

You have the opportunity of growing faster – you start from an existing base and can then develop it. With your own start up, you begin with nothing and growing can therefore take much longer.

Disadvantages

As I said earlier, this route into business can be fraught with difficulties, and these revolve around trying to avoid being saddled with a dog.

When Valerie was looking around for a business to buy she was offered an outlet in Staines. This place looked fine on paper, apparently producing some £25,000 profit each year out of sales of £125,000. She watched the shop from time to time over a period of two weeks, counting the number of people who went in. She multiplied up the figure she arrived at so that it represented an annualized estimate and divided that number into £125,000. Even if her estimates were out by as much as twice, either the customers were very rich artists or the owner's figure of £125,000 was somewhat overstated. Since 'very rich artists' is a contradiction in terms, she was inclined to doubt the word of the owner.

Many people liken buying a business to buying a home, and sometimes one is also buying a home. Moving house, and thus, in part, buying a home, is said to be one of the three biggest causes of stress in today's world, along with changing jobs and changing spouses. Think of all the awful things that can go wrong when you simply buy a house: there are so many factors to take into account many of which are ephemeral in nature (your family's perceptions of the property, for example). When buying a business, the problems can be ten or twenty times worse. Probably the reason why people do survive intact is because they are unaware; they rush in with their eyes tightly shut.

If it goes wrong you can rarely, if ever, take it back to the person who sold it to you. Here are just a few of the things that can go wrong:

- there may be little customer loyalty to outlet (although there may be a lot of loyalty to the owner) – and they move on;
- the business may be in the wrong location; and
- have assets which are really liabilities.

The major problem is that it is difficult to assess what you are actually buying – as much of the business is tied up with current owner.

Once you have bought the place, your problems are not over: it may be difficult to make changes to suit you – staff are used to doing things in the way they have been done in the past and may (no, will) resist your efforts to improve their productivity.

Ruth inherited an employee who often dealt with customers while Ruth was out of the office. She soon noticed that invoices for paltry amounts, well below her stated minimum charge, were being sent out. She found that her employee had agreed the prices with the customers because the employee felt 'guilty at charging them so much for so little work'.

Be of good cheer and stout heart (you will need it). There are some good opportunities which you could have a chance of buying.

Sources of opportunities

There are basically three different ways that you can find opportunities to buy. The first two are based on the fact that if someone wants to sell a business, they must make prospective purchasers aware of it, either by advertising or by placing it with an agent. The third, as ever involves you keeping your eyes and ears open, and, if you see a business you would like to buy, asking the owner if he or she wants to sell.

Adverts

One route for a vendor of business when looking for a buyer is to advertise. There are a number of publications which regularly carry advertisements of this kind.

Dalton's Weekly

Dalton's Weekly is a paper devoted to advertising of all sorts. Looking in the latest issue shows businesses from a chimney sweep, at £400, to a delicatessen at £6,500.

Exchange and Mart

Again, this is a publication consisting entirely of advertising. Businesses for sale can range between a small print business for £2,000 to a garage for £250,000.

National and local press

Many of the national and local press have 'Business to Business' pages which often contain adverts for businesses for sale.

Trade journals

There are a fairly large number of trade magazines for different types of businesses and these too sometimes carry businesses for sale.

Agents

Estate agents

Some vendors prefer to place their businesses in the hands of an agent, in much the same way that one would sell a house. In fact, it could be the same estate agent who handles both the house and the business. Many estate agents, especially town centre ones, have a commercial section. Sometimes this commercial arm will also sell businesses, and could well have a list of businesses which are currently on its books.

Business transfer agents

Business transfer agents are organizations which specialize in what their name implies; transferring businesses from their existing owners to new ones. The ones near you will be listed in the yellow pages.

Opportunity spotting

Opportunity spotting means that you simply watch out for businesses which you find attractive. Attractive in this sense is based on your own objectives, constraints and capabilities. After you have found what, to you, looks like a good proposition, ask the owner if he or she might be interested in selling. In many cases the answer will be a blank refusal, but you could hit on one which the owner was actively thinking of selling. You could even prompt that idea simply by asking. The owner may never have thought consciously about getting out until the opportunity presents itself.

Evaluating opportunities

In evaluating an opportunity to buy, the key words should be *do not hurry*.

> When George Duckett was looking to buy a shop, he
> was told by one vendor that if he wanted the place, he
> should make an offer in the next two days or the
> opportunity would be missed. The property was still
> on the market three months later.

There is absolutely no need to rush into making an offer – especially when the vendor tells you that he or she has other purchasers queueing up – if this were true, why should the vendor even be talking to you? Like so many things that the vendors of businesses are prone to claim, this, too, must be taken with an extremely large pinch of salt.

Try to see everything when looking round the prospect, especially, delve into dark corners. First impressions are worth quite a lot in buying a business. I emphasize that you should trust your first impressions when they tell you business is no good. But do not trust them in the reverse situation – professional help is definitely needed before you can make any realistic valuation of an opportunity. If you cannot arrive at a realistic value for the concern, you have no idea what a reasonable price for it might be. You will want a surveyor to evaluate the premises, an accountant to look at the businesses track record and assets, and a solicitor to make sure that the contract is not disadvantageous to you.

The first step in looking at such opportunities is to use the personal framework that you developed in Part I.

Using your personal framework

Hopefully, your framework will already be helping you in that you will by now only be looking at that type of business which fits. You need to ask;

- will it help achieve my goals,
- will my constraints allow me to do it (have I enough money, etc), and
- do I have the capacity to do it?

What to look for

There are a whole host of important factors you need to be looking for when looking round a proposed business, including:

- its shabbiness; it may look dented in some way – flaking paint, perhaps, and this can be a sign of the owner running out of the cash needed to maintain it.
- its location; which could be a very important factor in the business' future well-being. Its locality's characteristics could also be relevant.
- whether people can get to it easily: if it is not close to easy parking or other transport, it may not be right for you.
- what the staff look like; their initial greeting of you could tell you a lot about the business.
- does the stock appear to have been there a long time; a sure sign that things are not going well.

- very importantly, how much the business is dependent on the existing owner; his contacts, his friendships with regular customers who may be going to him because of that friendship rather than any other reason. This is going to be vital for the valuation of the business because if you think that it is heavily tied in to the owner, you can expect sales to drop sharply immediately you take over.

Information you can expect

To assess whether or not to buy you need some information beyond what your eyes and ears tell you. The two major things that should interest you in the early assessment stage are first, the owner's real reason for selling, and, second, the firm's track record – its figures.

Why selling

The reason why people are selling can tell you quite a lot about the business. Old age and illness are obviously good reasons for getting rid of a healthy business, and they can often be verified too, a major advantage from your point of view.

There are hundreds of other reasons which are not checkable by you, which is a major disadvantage to you. My fundamental question is why should anyone sell a business which is as good as the vendor claims? There are other ways of ridding oneself of the major responsibilities – putting in a manager, for example.

Their reasons for selling can be quite important to the purchase price or how the payments are made:

- suppliers pushing means that the owner might be happy for a fast cash deal; or
- a vendor who is retiring can wait for a good price but may be happy with deferred payments.

Try to find out how often has it changed hands, too – a business which has had several new owners could be a bad deal.

The figures

The company's financial track record will be shown in the accounts. Ask to be given a set of these for at least each of the last three years. They must be signed by an accountant with a reputable qualification before the smallest reliance can be placed on them. Where the business being considered is a sole trader or partnership, the accounts may be limited to a profit and loss account only, as opposed to a limited company where, as a prospective purchaser, you should also be able to get hold of a balance sheet as well.

The profit and loss account should tell you about things such as sales revenues. Vendors often claim to have suppressed sales revenue to keep it out of taxman's hands, in effect saying that the figure for sales revenues shown in the profit and loss account are lower than they really were. Never believe this claim – there is absolutely no way of checking its truth. If it is true, the vendor opens himself to a tip-off to the Inland Revenue (a common way for them to start investigating). He has no reason to believe that you will keep such facts to yourself. The profit and loss account should also give you the necessary and relevant information on gross profit, net profit and overheads, which you will need to weigh up your decision.

The balance sheet should give you an idea of the costs to the firm of its assets that are used to run the business, such as fittings; its debtors, the money it is owed by its customers; its creditors, the money owed to suppliers, and stocks.

These accounts will help you to assess the company's position: if it has a firm financial footing. Many people find it difficult to understand financial information, and if you are in this position, get help. Although you are trying to evaluate what will happen in the future, should you buy the place, the only facts you have to go on are past data – you must make the best use of them that you possibly can.

However, figures never tell the whole story. They say nothing of the fact that, perhaps, the staff are personable and friendly, or that there is an excellent working relationship with suppliers.

Price

When trying to work out what price should be paid you can use three approaches to help you arrive at a negotiating position. You can value all the assets separately and add the lot up. You can offer a price based on the amount of money it would cost to produce the same profits that the business under consideration does. Or you can offer simply what you can afford, where this is not in excess of the other two methods.

Asset based calculation

Adding up the various market values of the assets on offer gives you a minimum price: if you were to pay this figure, you could then sell on the assets separately, at no loss to yourself. Mind you, the vendor could also sell the assets piecemeal at these values, and thus has no reason to sell them as a package to you at this price. Hence it becomes the very bottom price of the range of acceptable prices. You will need independent valuations of stock and of the premises.

There is usually no market value for other assets which might be bought – as a guide to the resale value of assets where few buyers exist for that asset, a bank would use only 20% of the cost of the asset. Look also at how old the assets are and when you would have to replace them, working out how much that will cost. Get your accountant to help you value the debtors, if you are also taking them over – not all will pay you.

Profits based calculation

Here, you are trying to work out how much you would have to invest if you were to get a profit stream equivalent to that which this business produces. It involves an assessment of the value of the business' goodwill with its customers and staff. Because such things are so intangible, this method usually ends up being a simple multiple of the average profits produced over the last three years. A common multiple is three times the profit.

Problems occur with this, as who is to say what should be included or excluded from profit, which average should be taken, and what is the appropriate multiple to use?

How much can you afford

Using this as a guide, you must first determine what the maximum you could afford is, based on your estimates of the business' likely future cash flows and profits, taking into account any interest you will be paying. This gives you price ceiling above which it would not be sensible to go.

Hidden costs

Finally, there are the costs which everyone forgets to take into account. Accountants, laywers and surveyors rarely work for the love of it and thus you are in for some pretty hefty professional fees.

In fact, it is not as simple as it sounds. Do take professional help. You will need it.

Chapter Ten:
Franchises

Keith Lord was looking for a business idea. In his search he visited the Franchise Exhibition and saw the Adventure Game concept. This is an adventure war-game played by adults in open country and woodland. He had no previous experience of organizing anything similar, but found it an attractive idea and something he might like to do. He arranged with The Great Adventure Game to take out a franchise and he launched the Great Adventure Game (Bedford) in April 1987.

Franchising represents a tremendous route for the creation of a business for a certain type of person, especially those with little experience of running their own businesses. There are some 15,000 franchised outlets employing 169,000 people in the UK. It represents a way into business where the generation of ideas of one's own is unnecessary. Here you take somebody else's well developed idea and open up a 'branch' of the business which you personally own. It is a superb route to owning your own business and the opportunities for franchising are growing ever wider. However there are certain considerations, advantages, and disadvantages that need to be looked at. You also need to know where to find franchise opportunities and how to check them out once you've found them.

Franchising: What Is It?

In 1986 Karl Gibbons founded Flash Trash, a chain of ladies' accessory shops. His first three shops, which he personally owns, are in Regent Street, Brighton and Kingston Upon Thames. He plans to open three more of his own but he also plans to have a chain of thirty to forty outlets three years from now. Were he to buy all thirty shops himself he would need many millions of pounds in up front capital and consequently he decided that outlets number seven onwards would be franchised. The outlets he owns began trading in late 1986 and early 1987 and have proved extremely successful, not just in central London.

He has invited people to participate in this business as franchisees. He will allow people to set up in, say, Milton Keynes under the Flash Trash label and copying the Flash Trash success factors in other ways. The franchisee in Milton Keynes will set up a shop with a pre-designed Flash Trash store front selling Flash Trash products, bought from Karl. The franchisee will take the profits of the business which Karl estimates in the first year at £25,000.

In return the franchisee gives Karl an initial fee of £8,500, a royalty on sales of 3%, and Karl makes some profit on his sales of the basic product to his franchisee.

This example encapsulates franchising, and is called the 'business format franchise'. Here the franchisor (Karl), from his earlier experience in running his own outlets, gives the franchisee an entire idea or concept. He also shows how it will operate in practice. The franchisor licenses the franchisee to use his already developed name and/or trade mark.

In return the franchisee agrees to pay in three ways for the privilege.

He is expected to pay an initial investment,

a royalty on sales, and

in buying his goods for resale from the franchisor he will be increasing the franchisor's profits.

In addition to allowing the franchisee to trade under his name, the franchisor usually provides some form of backup. This may take the form of advertising and promotion of the name on a national basis. He may also bear the cost of some local advertising: Karl allocates one sixth of the royalty back to advertising in the local area. He usually gives some business advice pre and post launch and he has often set up lines of credit which the franchisee will be able to access. He will undoubtedly want to help the franchisee regarding the location of the outlet and may help in negotiating the lease. There are often predetermined accounting and stock control systems which can help both the franchisor and the franchisee.

In addition to all the above the franchisor often provides training or education for the franchisee in how to run this particular sort of outlet.

The franchisee actually owns the franchise and can sell it should he want to, but in reality the businesses are intertwined, although legally separate. The franchisee and the franchisor depend on each other in many ways in making profits. The franchisor usually reserves the right of first refusal when the franchisee wants to sell the business. He often wants to be able to approve any subsequent purchaser.

The advantages

Sally Jones, an engineer, wanted to set up a Wimpy
franchise in Leatherhead some years ago. She realized
that the outlet was likely to be profitable from day one
and capable of being run by someone with no background in fast food, given that Wimpy would train her.

The major benefit of franchises is that there is a much higher chance of success
than with your own business idea. Some recent research showed that business
format franchise failure rates were as little as 7% in 1986 and expected to fall
to 4% for 1987. This compares to 67% in the general business start-up world.
There are a number of reasons for this and the most important are that:

- the concept has been tested and found to work. The owner would not
  be able to sell the franchises if this were not true. As usual there are
  exceptions – the cowboys.
- the franchisor has been through the learning curve and should have
  ironed out most of the early start-up hitches and thus can help the
  franchisee overcome set-up problems.
- the name is already known in the market place and may also be known
  to the people who supply materials necessary to provide the service.

It is in the franchisor's interests to help the franchisee create a successful
business and consequently will help the franchisee in a number of different
ways. This help is usually not available to those setting up businesses from
ideas generated by themselves:

- There is someone to turn to in case you need help. This cannot be
  overrated. It certainly is not available to those starting their own
  businesses from scratch. In fact this problem is cited by many business
  people as one of the things they most dislike about running their own
  firms.
- The franchisor usually provides training for the franchisee in running
  the business and consequently you do not need specific skills.
- You inherit valuable business systems. The franchisor will be interested in keeping a record of your sales (his royalty is based on it) and
  of your stock levels. Basically this is done for the franchisor's benefit
  but also has major benefits from the franchisee's point of view.

All the cash registers in Flash Trash outlets are con-
nected to the central computer in the head office. This

allows Karl to keep the daily record of sales amongst other things, but more importantly allows him to identify fast moving items of stock and, therefore, helps the franchisee keep a reasonable stock level.

Many small firms go out of business because of inadequate financial control. They often lack financial control because they do not keep records. If you are forced, via the franchise agreement, to keep records then at least this will not be one of your problems.

You also have an immediate peer group. The other franchisees in the chain will want to meet and talk from time to time about their problems in operation. And as there are usually geographical limits on each outlet's sales, the franchisees are not usually in competition. This means that they can share their problems openly and can often help each other. Again this is unavailable to anyone starting their business from scratch, and is also cited as a problem for many small business people.

The franchisor often arranges with banks to provide finance for franchisees. This is usually a loan over a number of years amounting to two-thirds of the required capital. Most of the big banks now have specialist franchising units and they too have recognised the high success rates of franchised outlets, and consequently are willing to put more money on the line for this type of operation than they usually do for new businesses.

Design costs are reduced.

Edmund Bradley set up a pick and mix sweets outlet as an in-store concession in the Birmingham Hamleys. The largest single component of the set up cost of the business, called Jamboree, was the design cost.

Because the franchisor has already paid for the design and will want you as the franchisee to follow his logos, trade marks, name and concepts the design costs are reduced in relation to other business ideas.

It is possible that the franchising route might actually be cheaper than setting up yourself. On your own you are certain to make mistakes in the early stages of your business. Many people say that for the first twelve months you simply don't know where you are. For the second twelve months you are correcting the mistakes you made in the first twelve months and it is only in the third year that you actually start to have a viable business. These early mistakes might prove expensive. Hopefully, the franchisor will have overcome these problems before you ever become his franchisee and thus these costs won't be incurred by you.

The franchisor usually limits the geographical trading of each outlet. This means that you as a franchisee have a guaranteed protected market place.

The franchisor usually wants to stay abreast of the market place and will consequently bring in new designs, products, trade marks, logos, and so on. You as franchisee will benefit from this.

> The Flash Trash recently introduced Extra Flash. This is a range of young British designer accessories, at the leading edge of ladies fashion. This range sells well.

Many business people agonize over the purchase of the 'right' equipment and fittings. You as a franchisee will not have these agonies because the franchisor will help you decide what to buy.

It is possible that the franchisor will pass on the benefits of his strength in buying to the franchisee.

It is again in the franchisor's interest to help with site location and selection. In fact he may insist on a veto of the premises that you have chosen on the basis of your poor choice (in his view).

The franchisee may benefit from the activities of the franchisor in respect of publicity.

> The name of Flash Trash and photographs of the product being worn by models have appeared in many ladies' journals and newspapers.

The disadvantages

Given that there are so many advantages to the franchising of businesses, why is the whole world not comprised entirely of franchised outlets? Well, there are some problems.

The first and most important is that although you can make a good living from franchised outlets there are no fast megabucks to be made for the franchisee. This not true for the franchisor – his earnings are unlimited.

The second major problem is the cost of the franchised outlet, in terms of the initial investment and of the royalty paid. The royalty is based on sales and can vary quite dramatically from one franchisor to another. For example, The royalty on sales for Flash Trash is 3% and that for Kall-Kwik Printing is 10%.

There would not be a problem if the level of sales revenue was entirely in the control of either the franchisee or the franchisor. In fact the level of sales is affected by both sides to the agreement. It is perfectly possible that the franchisor may want to reduce price to increase turnover and whilst this might increase sales revenue it doesn't always mean an increase in profit. In such circumstances the franchisor would benefit but not the franchisee. Again the franchisee may consider that his turnover is almost entirely due to his own advertising and promotional efforts, with very little coming from the advertising promotional efforts of the franchisor. In other words, if one of the parties to the agreement is not pleased, there could well be arguments.

Some other effects to consider include the high standards that the franchisor will require the franchisee to keep. There will be tight control over product quality in the materials used in the provision of the product or service. There could well be regular inspections.

There is also little scope for individual initiative, in the major areas of the business, given that the franchisor has licensed an entire concept. For example, the franchisee will almost certainly not be allowed to sell any products outside the franchisor's range. And the franchisee has little or no recourse against the franchisor should the franchisor start doing things that damage the business. Finally, because the franchisor takes a profit on the goods he sells the franchisee for resale or for use in the business, the franchisee may well be paying above market rates for these goods.

Where to find franchising opportunities

The number of franchising opportunities is growing every day as people with successful businesses look to expand them. There are a number of ways that you can see these opportunities for yourself.

Perhaps the best method, having identified the things you do and don't want to do, is to look around for businesses that appear to be successful, and which you think could well work elsewhere.

> The original franchisee of Tie Rack saw the opportunity first whilst walking across the concourse of one of London's major stations. He saw a Tie Rack outlet in operation and was stunned by its tremendous marketing focus and attractiveness to customers. He had never heard of nor seen Tie Rack before but tracked down its owner, Steve Bishko, and asked if Steve would be interested in franchising an outlet. Tie Rack was by then only a year old and had never franchised anything. He became its first, and eventually largest, franchisee.

British Franchise Association

The British Franchise Association[1] (BFA) is the trade association for franchisors and as such can provide information about franchise opportunities. It also acts as a professional body for franchisors, laying down a code of ethics. This will allow you to check out a franchisor against what is considered to be 'good practice'.

Other sources

There are a number of other sources where you can find out information about franchises. There is the National Franchisers Exhibition in October each year, sponsored by the British Franchise Association. There are also the Enterprise series of exhibitions operated by Acumex Ltd.[2] There are many Franchise opportunities here.

There is an excellent book called *Taking up a Franchise*[3] by Godfrey Golzen and Colin Barrow. This has a tremendous amount of information in it regarding the advantages/disadvantages of taking up a franchise, evaluating a franchise, the Franchise Contract, financing a franchise, legal and tax considerations, and acts as a guide to opportunities.

Finally there are some franchising magazines. These are *The Franchise Magazine*[4] and *Franchise World*[5] and are both extremely useful.

Checking out a franchise

In franchising, as in any other area, there are people willing to part fools from their money. Where you get people happy to pay large amounts of initial fees to a franchisor you are certain to get a number of cowboys, taking the up front money with little or no return. You, therefore, need to check out the proposition and the opportunity really thoroughly before parting with any money.

What is expected of the franchisee by the franchisor, and vice versa, is laid down in the Franchise Contract. This document details your rights to the product, name, trade marks, logos, and soon, it will outline what will be expected of you. It should lay out what you can expect of the franchisor in return for your initial fee, royalty and any other payments. It is central to the

---

1   British Franchise Association, Franchise Chambers, 75a Bell Street, Henley-on-Thames, Oxfordshire RG9 2BD Tel: 0491 578049.
2   Acumex Ltd, Drewitt House, 865 Ringwood Road, Bournemouth, Dorset BH11 8LW Tel (0202) 581122.
3   *Taking up a Franchise* – 3rd Edition Godfrey Golzen & Colin Barrow, Kogan Page.
4   The Franchise Magazine, Franchise Development Services Ltd, Castle House, Norwich NR2 1PJ. Tel: (0603) 62301.
5   Franchise World, James House, 37 Nottingham Road, London SW17 7EA Tel: (01) 767 1371.

checking out of a franchise opportunity, and you must get your lawyers working on the contract if you are serious in taking up any particular opportunity. However, there are many things you can do before you reach the point at which you need to get legal advice.

The most important thing is to check the viability of the operation you are looking at. Later chapters in this book will help you. Some of the major considerations you need to take into account are as follows:

- Is this the sort of sales outlet which will achieve the franchisors sales targets?
- What will happen in profitability terms if you miss a sales forecast by 10%? 25%? 50%?
- Is the location of the outlet good?
- Are there sufficient traffic flows, either by foot or car?
- Is the sort of labour you need easily available in the area?
- What happens if you discover you are unsuited to the type of business?
- What happens if you are seriously ill or die?
- What will be the effect on profitability for cash flows if the local authority increase the rates by 25%? 50%?
- Is the area sufficiently well served by local media?
- Can you communicate effectively with your chosen target?

Go and see other franchisees in the same business. Ask the franchisor to point out one or two of them but also find one or two of your own. Obviously, he's well recommend ones who will speak favourably of him. The other franchisees will usually be willing to talk to you because it's unlikely that you will be in direct competition with them, and you may well become a colleague. In fact, it is amazing what information they may let slip.

A couple of years ago I was helping George Hale check out a franchise opportunity. We decided to go and talk to the Maidenhead franchisee, as Maidenhead was a similar sort of town to the one in which George had been offered an outlet. He was tremendously helpful. He even showed us his monthly management accounts for the past twelve months from which we were able to get an excellent idea of both turnover levels and seasonality. Naturally, the data also allowed us to check wage levels, cost of the goods for resale, and profitability. He was also able to help in easing one of George's major worries in the operation of his own outlet, that of using part-time labour. The Maidenhead visit was immensely helpful in the subsequent negotiations and eventual launch of George's outlet.

You need to check out the franchisor as well as checking out other franchise outlets. Look at his most recent accounts in Companies House,[1] which you can copy yourself from the microfiche.

In addition to his financial data you will need to ask:

- How long has he been trading?
- How many outlets does he personally own?
- How many franchised outlets are there?
- What is his background in?

You need to know something about the service/concept/idea and goods for resale, if there are any. You must satisfy yourself that the concept has been tried and tested elsewhere, preferably in an area similar to yours. You at least must find it fun to do. If you don't think you're going to enjoy it, don't go into it!

However many considerations there might be, it remains an excellent route into business for yourself. It also represents a good way of acquiring well-above-average earnings and high satisfaction, with a relatively low risk.

---

[1] Companies House, 55 City Road, London EC1.

Chapter Eleven:
Management Buy-outs

A few years ago the general manager of a division of
the British Oxygen Company (BOC), Robert Wright,
spotted the opportunity for buying-out the division
which he managed. The division concerned, called
Advanced Welding Products, was part of an operating
unit that BOC, for its own reasons, wanted to divest
itself of. Robert approached a number of colleagues to
find out if they would be interested in joining. They
were, he then approached a potential investor and also
got support. A package was put together for £175,000.

Introduction

As you can see from the example, a management buy-out takes place when a
group of managers make a bid for part of their employer's business. Spicer &
Pegler, a large firm of accountants, describe it as

> 'A transaction by which management of a business
> acquires a substantial stake in, and frequently effective
> control of, the business which it formerly managed,
> usually by means of financial arrangements tailored to
> suit individuals of relatively modest means'.

In fact, the new management team usually has voting control, although they
will have to give significantly large percentages of the equity to the financial
backers. The previous employer usually has no, or at least, an insignificant
shareholding. As an economic phenomenon, it is a re-marrying of ownership
and control.

Think about the ownership of any large publicly quoted company. No one
individual is normally sufficiently wealthy to own a majority shares-holding.
The ownership of the shares, therefore, is likely to be diverse. The law says

that the shareholders own the company but, where the shareholders are many in number, this approach falls down. When you own an asset you expect to be able to use it and certainly to control it. Why bother having a boat? Some would argue that those people who control an asset, are those who actually own it in any real sense.

Who owns large public companies? If you see the concept of ownership as control, then the shareholders do not seem to be owners at all. It is the directors and the top management team who appear as 'owner', since they control the company. They are self perpetuating too – they decide who their successors are. Buy-outs reverse this trend, anyway, temporarily.

There are a range of different structures and deals which might be called buy-outs or are in some way associated with them. These are:

- the traditional buy-out, as described above;
- the levered buy-out, which is the situation where the management 'lever' their investment in shares by taking on large chunks of debt instead of buying shares in real terms;
- the buy-in, which can be the same as the previous examples, but where the management team taking over are outsiders;
- the spin-off, where a team of employees take over part of the assets and workforce of the parent;
- a second type of spin-off, fairly common in high technology, where the parent encourages an employee to set up a new venture, or to develop new technologies.

The last two represent excellent opportunities for those of you who want your own business but are not in a position to drive a buy-out forward. Spin-offs are considered separately in the next chapter.

The commonest size of buy-out is in the £1 million to £2 million range but they can be both very small or very large.

> Dudley Fisher decided to change the emphasis of his business and as a result his car spares retail operation (one shop) became peripheral to his interests. The shop manager recognized this and suggested to Dudley that he should buy it. As Dudley wanted to expand into new areas and needed cash, he agreed. The price was negotiated at £30,000.

> In 1981 the National Freight company was sold to its employees for £53.5 million. Those employees who were involved in the buy-out, have since made a fortune.

National Freight has been eclipsed since by deals such as Mardon Packaging (£73 million) and the US, naturally, has seen much larger buy-outs: Safeway was priced in billions.

The buy-out phenomenon first started in the US. The interest began in the mid-1970s, and has simply taken off. There was so much interest by potential investors that the buy-in was spawned as a response to the lack of good buy-out opportunities when compared to the amount of money available. It has been suggested that the growth of buy-outs has been fuelled by an increasing awareness by managers themselves that such things are possible. Without this awareness there would be far fewer buy-outs because the opportunities would simply be missed. An increasing preparedness on the part of investors to back buy-outs has also increased the opportunities. This is absolutely vital and may well have come about, in part, because of the increased number of 'exit routes' that are now available. An exit route is a path to realization or sale of the original investment. Routes such as the Unlisted Securities Market (USM) and the Third Market simply did not exist ten years ago, neither did the ability of the firm itself to buy back its own shares. USM flotations are becoming very attractive to investors. A political environment which actively encourages enterprise not least through increased privatization has also fuelled an increase in buy-outs. And, finally, a burgeoning move by large companies towards focused activities, rather than conglomerates, combined with a better understanding of the benefits of buy-outs, as compared with other forms of divestment has also helped.

There are three sides to any buy-out triangle. The person or team who wants to buy-out, the current employer (and hence potential vendor), and anyone who might wish to invest in the company all need to be considered when you check out a possible buy-out opportunity. Each of the players have different benefits and drawbacks, some in conflict, which will affect the likelihood of whether a buy-out chance exists or not.

First, look at the benefits from the employer or vendor's point of view. When a company wants to sell part of itself it must open up to an examination by prospective purchasers, some of whom may be competitors. There is an excellent chance that the employees will get to know about it and lose interest, possibly being tempted away to more secure jobs. Certainly the unit about to be sold will become less efficient. Arranging a buy-out can save all of this. It can save money too, in that there are no agents fees or commissions and it is a way of safeguarding loyalty.

It is not all sweetness and light for the vendor, or we would have seen more. The vendor will probably not end up with a price as high as they might otherwise have achieved because they have only one potential customer. In fact, it has been known for a vendor to encourage a management bid just to up the price from another bidder. Steer well clear of this situation because the management team are on a hiding to nothing; because, unless their bid succeeds they are out on their ears.

For the manager who starts the wheels in motion, and the team he surrounds himself with, money is not initially the main motivation. The fact is that the challenge of taking on full, independent responsibility for the bought-out unit is far stronger. It can be a route to becoming wealthy and it is certainly a short-cut to owning your own business, but autonomy is likely to mean more than that in the early stages.

It is not a bed of roses for the management team either. There is a lot of personal sacrifice, long hours and hard decisions ahead. It is not easy, the pressures are strong and it can be risky. Many buy-out managers have to make personal financial commitment to the venture, often involving their family homes; this is a risk and you can lose it all in the event of the business' failure.

For one person, everything is an easy ride – the financial backer. They would not agree with me, because buy-outs do fail and they can get their fingers burnt like anyone else. The fact remains, however, that buy-outs are not generally as risky as other opportunities available to institutions which invest in buy-outs. The managing director of the venture capital arm of a major bank mentioned that he had a portfolio split roughly 50:50 between buy-outs and 'straight' venture capital. He expects the buy-out portfolio to out-perform the remainder by a factor of five to one – not because the returns on the buy-out investments are higher (they are roughly similar), but because of the higher failure rate of the ordinary investments.

As a caveat, great care is needed – can your employer keep you on after it knows you want to buy out? Your allegiance is now in question. Even if your offer is considered seriously you will cause tremendous potential aggravation to arise such as jealousy at the prospect of your making a success. Who will you leave behind? Your boss? His or her boss? Imagine their reaction to having part of their empire cut away. In the past your objectives and your employers were not necessarily in conflict – they are now. You want to minimise the price you will have to pay and they want to maximise it. You are now hostile and a possible danger to the parent.

Your relationship with your employer is not the only personal factor you will have to consider during a buy-out opportunity. You may have to take an entire workforce, or even worse, perhaps, only part of a workforce. What about the workers? Will the people who really do the work be happy moving from a reasonably secure base to an insecure future? You must consider whether or not there will be advantages and benefits from their point of view.

How To Spot An Opportunity

Opportunities for buy-outs occur when there is some sort of dissatisfaction between the company and the operating unit which might be bought out. Dissatisfaction in this sense can come in a variety of forms. There are a number of studies and some research into why companies allow buy-outs and these point the way to creating a framework through which one can assess whether a buy-out opportunity exists.

In looking at whether a buy-out is possible consider if your employer is in one of the following situations:

- being privatized. This can offer employees many chances for buying-out;
- unprofitable subsidiaries, no longer mainstream business, or simply political factors;
- parent being liquidated. Companies like this can have many profitable subdivisions;
- a family run business with succession problems. If there are no obvious successors in the chain the company's owners may be happy to let it go as a going concern to the managers (they will get a better price).

One study[1] suggests that the following may cause divestment. Firstly, a remote geographical location; where the subsidiary and parent are physically distant problems arise in all sorts of areas, including supply of materials but probably more importantly, in the relationship between the two managements. Secondly, a lack of strategic fit; quite often companies end up owning operating units which have no real benefits to their mainstream activities. This might happen through the takeover of a subsidiary which itself has other operating divisions. In addition, there is a move towards greater focus in business, with the idea of conglomerates losing favour in the markets. Companies like this may well want to divest parts of their empires in the search for better focus. Problems elsewhere in a company can also cause divestment. Where this happens the management's attention may well be taken up for quite long periods elsewhere and allowing a buy-out under such circumstances could well be a boon in freeing up time. Bad management too can lead to a possible opportunity. It is perfectly possible that the operating unit you have your eye on arrived in its current state through the poor capabilities of the people currently in control. If you are thinking of making a proposal in such circumstances, be very careful about what you say to whom.

A previous bad acquisition may produce opportunities, too, as acquiring companies is very much like acquiring a spouse – there is a courtship, a wedding and a honeymoon. After the honeymoon is over there is a relationship which, like any other marriage, has to be worked at if it is to flower and be enjoyable for both sides. Sometimes it does not work out, not least for reasons of 'psychological distance', where the ethos that runs through the two firms is too far apart. Then the opportunity for divorce appears. Do you want to be the third party cited in the divorce courts? Finally, low growth or poor prospects is another potential area where divestment may occur. This can happen to any part of a business at any time, simply through changing market

---

1   Boddewynn J. J. *International Divestment*, Business International, 1976.

conditions. It may present an opportunity, especially where the buy-out team can slim down the unit after buying-out, it then disposes of unnecessary overheads in the process.

Whether or not an opportunity exists for you, as opposed to an opportunity for someone else, probably depends on your position with your employer. Do you have line responsibility for any particular activity within the firm? If you do, is it separable from the mainstream activities of your company? If you are currently dissatisfied in any way it might be symptomatic of one of the factors which cause opportunities for divestment.

In fact, the majority of people reading this will not be in that position and consequently will have no opportunity for themselves directly. Take heart – you do not necessarily have to be the person in charge. If you see the type of activity which would lend itself to buying-out, approach the person who currently runs it to try to get their enthusiasm and leadership. Be careful you do not get fired in the process!

You also need to look at the physical and financial position of the operating unit. You are actually checking to see how easily separable the unit is in relation to its parent. Does it have its own facilities or is it simply tucked away in a large factory? If the former then it will be easier to separate. How tied in to the parent's accounting system is the unit? Is it a profit centre? If it is, it will be easier to assess whether you can make it profitable.

Who To Turn To

If you want to look more closely at the idea you will need to talk to a number of people early on in the process. These are your team, professional advisors and an investor (to see if finance is likely).

Your Team

The team you create around you is a deciding factor in whether or not a buy-out can be successful. This is certainly true when looking to see if anyone will finance the proposition. One venture capitalist was recently heard to say:

> the three most important factors in a buy-out are: the management team, the management team and the management team, in that order.'

Consequently, when examining the idea, you need to look at the people that you might be able to persuade to come with you. They will need to have commitment to the new business, a range of skills which complement your own and the ability to work as part of a team when under pressure.

Big pressures build up both before and after – thus team selection is vital. All teams start with only one person, namely you. In exactly the same way as suggested earlier in the book, your personal objectives and characteristics are very important. You need to be able to review your personal strengths and weaknesses, so as to be able to determine the type of other characteristics you need in a team.

The pressures that a buy-out creates can be enormous. Beforehand, they are caused by such factors as the:

- parent company's attitude to people who have suddenly become 'suspect';
- antagonism that invariably exists in the people who will suffer, in a corporate sense, from the move;
- envy that that is created;
- fact that the team may have to lay their own resources on the line;
- fact that the team are operating in secret for much of the time;
- fear of the unknown.

Afterwards, pressures can result from:

- psychological changes which are necessary to move from being a corporate manager to an owner. These changes can be quite large;
- operating with far fewer resources than previously;
- having to make hard decisions regarding people who might have been friends under the earlier regime;
- the loneliness which the owners of any business suffer;
- the far greater need for their decisions and actions to be right, and preferably right first time.

Lastly, getting rid of a team member after the event is a major problem. You need to get it right first time, which increases the pressure on you.

Professional advisors

You can usually get free advice early in the process from a top class accounting firm. They will often give the first consulting session free in any case, but with you they might be looking at a new and possibly lucrative client. You do need accountants, preferably not from the same firm as your parent company uses.

Your needs will include looking at the financial aspects of the buy-out. Choose a firm with experience of buy-outs. The top firms are probably best for your purposes – their experience, networks and the quality of advice.

Although the cost can be high, the cost of getting the buy-out wrong will be much higher, both in financial and in personal terms. Choose someone you can work with on a personal level as you will be spending a lot of time together.

The investor

An initial approach is necessary to find out if the proposition is likely to get as far as the financing stage. This approach should be made prior to any firm commitment to the employer. Where do you get advice like this? The best place to start is probably your own bank manager who will put you in touch with the venture capital arm of the bank. You do not have to stick with them if they prove valueless, in fact getting two or three investors involved so that they can compete is always useful.

The proposal

The offer, subject to contract, is the first step in the official proposal. This usually goes to the managing director, in the form of a letter laying out the initial offer, but you need quite a lot of input before this stage. If your accountants and potential investor are experienced in buy-outs they will be able to help tremendously in negotiating an offer. For one thing, your accountants will be better able to judge what the unit might be worth than you are yourself. You must not forget that 'worth' and 'value' are very subjective things – what is 'worth'? What means a lot to one person has a negligible value to another. Always remember that your offer has to fit in with the objectives of the parent company.

> Remember Robert and BOC? His offer failed, not because the money was not enough. His offer of £175,000 was higher than the price that the company finally sold Advanced Welding Products to. It was sold to another tiny company, GEC. The reason was that the customers of AWP were also large users of gas and BOC did not want to upset these customers by selling AWP to an 'unreliable' buyer. Robert thinks that the buy-out offer was an embarrassing irrelevance so far as BOC is concerned.

You may prefer to have an independent advisor helping in the negotiations as you and your team will be in a weak position. The advisor might be able to get a better price.

There are many things to consider including; the details of the scheme and financing pack, the teams' shares, retaining customers, retaining suppliers, tax planning.

The money

If you have a good proposition you should be able to find the money quite easily – venture capitalists lust after good buy-outs. Try to talk to at least three potential backers in the initial stages. That way you are less likely to be stitched up.

You will need a business plan to get any money. The plan's major advantage is that it helps you and the team to plan the company's future and thus make the mistakes on paper rather than with your money. However, it also serves as a way of raising money. It shows the strengths and weaknesses of the strategy and also covers the opportunities and threats facing the new unit.

The business plan should cover areas such as these:

– Executive summary;
– The Company – current status, short term objectives, medium/long term objectives, the management team, the management's objectives;
– Markets and Competition – current market, user benefits, customer benefits, market projections, competition, forecast market share, segments, sales strategy;
– The Products and Manufacturing – applications, performance, present set up, further requirements, patents, labour;
– Selling – current position, future changes, pricing;
– Financials – history, funding requirements, forecasts, sensitivity analysis;
– Appendices – management team CVs, brochures/photos/visuals.

When you are talking about business plans you need to understand that presentation is very important – you can judge a book by the cover.

Getting finance for anything requires an act of faith on behalf of the backer. If you are to raise money successfully you need to understand what will make any particular backer have faith in you. In commercial lending, your bank manager's profit lies in the interest he earns on his loan to you, and, therefore, he is interested in your profitability only in so far as it is sufficient to cover the interest due. Obviously, he will not make any money if you go out of business, so he is necessarily interested in the viability of your business for the duration of any loan.

People financing a buy-out differ in a big way from your High Street bank manager. For one thing they are dealing in much larger sums. The real difference lies in the fact that they will want a 'piece of the action', ie, some shares. Their big returns will come from the capital gains when they sell their shares. Consequently they are very interested in profits because profits will help the share price.

However that is only half the story. To be able to make any gain at all they have to have an 'exit' route, that is somewhere to sell their shares. There are three traditional exit routes; a stock market launch, a trade sale, or selling to the original team.

You need to be able to show any potential investor that there will be an exit route. Incidentally, the most common route is the trade sale; which involves selling to a larger company which has an interest in your type of business, say, one of your larger customers. How will you enjoy having a corporate big brother with a minority, but significant, shareholding?

The investors will be looking for opportunities which will return some five or ten times their original investment after about five years, and you will need to remember that when assessing buy-out opportunities. The idea must therefore be capable of rapid growth.

You do not always need venture capital, ordinary bank lending might suffice, especially if combined with your own wealth. In fact you sometimes need no wealth of your own. The following example is true, although I have changed the names:

> Steve, the marketing manager of a manufacturer of pressure gauges, and John, the design and production manager, were dissatisfied with their employer because they felt that they had not received the recognition that they felt they deserved (directorships). They decided to set up in competition with their employer who they felt was ignoring certain profitable segments. Their research was excellent and supported the view that there was a marketplace which they could exploit and they arranged with a German manufacturer to supply the first products. Their intention was to use John's skills and manufacture the product themselves after they had proved the market. They did all of this in their spare time whilst continuing to work for their company.
>
> The time came to hand in their notices – both resigning themselves to the fact that they would not have their cars, offices and jobs at the end of that day. In the company's position, they would have had themselves out of the building immediately.
>
> When the managing director, Peter, heard their stories he told them not to be too hasty and said that as they were the core of the management team, the company might not survive their departure. By the end

of the day they still had their cars and offices, but were on the verge of becoming the new owners of the business, rather than simply employees. Peter had persuaded the parent that this subsidiary would go out of business if the person who had all the customer loyalty, Steve, and the person who had the manufacturing track record, John, left. Would they be willing to do a deal? They were.

With the help of one of the top ten firms of accountants, they put together a deal which allowed the subsidiary to buy back its own shares from the parent, borrowing the money from the bank against the subsidiary's assets, and re-issuing them in equal parts to Steve, John and (surprise, surprise) Peter.

Steve and John are now owners of two-thirds of the business for which they were simply employees. Naturally they got their directorships. And all without using any of their own money.

The Buy-In

The buy-in may be the coming thing in the tools available to institutions interested in financing venture development. Essentially it consists of an institution backing a management team from outside the 'target' company. It arises from the fact that there are not enough good buy-outs for the institutions to invest in, and hence investors have to create their own opportunities.

Situations where a buy-in might be worthwhile are:

- family businesses with succession problems;
- enterprising businesses which have management deficiencies;
- the failing companies from an institution's books which could be either buy-outs or straight venture capital.

The target companies may even be hostile to the buy-in. Obviously, the team is even more important under these circumstances than in the buy-out. To take advantage of this growing area you would need to be seen as a very versatile and ambitious high-flyer, not just in your own company, but in the financial world in general.

The aftermath

The opportunity you might be looking for must be able to stand a certain amount of neglect. Secret meetings, arranging finance, making an offer and all the other, very time consuming activities will mean that you and your team will have had to be away from the day-to-day management of the unit. It will now need to be picked up and turned around the way you think it ought to be. Even if the bid fails, there will be an aftermath – you will never be able to regain the old status quo.

For Robert Wright the move may have been beneficial in the long term: Robert went with AWP to GEC along with the others in AWP's management team. Within twelve months, they, the five top managers led by Robert, had left AWP. Robert attributes this to two reasons;

- the changed aspirations of the management team – they had wanted to be free of BOC, but were now managers in GEC, and
- the different ethos within GEC which they were not used to.

In fact, the team, again led by Robert, set up a new company together. This company is called Synergic Interactive Systems Limited and sells advanced welding systems.

Chapter Twelve:
Corporate Spin-Offs

Introduction

This route to owning your own business may prove to be better for many than corporate buy-outs. You may not be the manager of a transferable unit, you might not be able to get the finance or build a team. In fact, where a buy-out opportunity exists there are normally relatively few people in the organization who can take advantage of it.

There are any number of different types of spin-off but this chapter will concentrate on two main areas, which are the full sponsored spin-off and hive off.

The full sponsored spin-off is where you, an employee, see an opportunity for making a successful business, often springing out of the activities you are involved in for your employer, but not necessarily in the mainstream of their business. Such opportunities quite frequently occur as off shoots of research of some kind. Commonly one sees this phenomenon in high-tech industries, probably because they are aware of the possibility rather than because the opportunities do not exist elsewhere.

Martin Brown studied for a BA in Business Studies at Thames Polytechnic and, as part of his training, spent a year working for a supplier of veterinary medical products – a wholesaler of a range of products rather than a manufacturer. As part of his work for them he had to complete a market research project, one part of which showed that a strong demand existed for a product which no one manufactured. This was a more convenient type of horse bandage. One of his report conclusions was that his employer should start to manufacture this product. They turned this opportunity down, probably quite sensibly, since they were a sales, not manufacturing, oriented company. However, they did fail to see another opportunity for themselves – that of sponsoring Martin in the manufacture of the product. He went back to finish his degree but did not forget the idea and subsequently came to Cranfield to develop it into a business for himself. He got his first sales in November 1987 and, perhaps obviously, has earned himself the soubriquet 'Horse Doctor', although he trades under the name Bosney Bandages.

The hive-off of part of a company's activities is also an area where just about anyone in the organization can get a business going. As an example look at George Worthington.

George used to work in the typesetting division of a group of local newspapers. The company felt it could get its typesetting done more effectively by using subcontractors and persuaded George that he could take on that rôle. The company gave George the machinery and made the workforce redundant, where-upon they moved en masse to George, as agreed. He won the contract and now has a company typesetting for the company which used to employ him. In fact, it is his only customer.

Fully sponsored spin-offs

An example of a fully sponsored spin-off is Domino Ink Jet Printers.

In 1978 Graham Mintoe spun Domino Ink Jet Printers out of Cambridge Consultants Ltd (CCL), itself a subsidiary of Arthur D Little. CCL is a high tech consultancy but Graham wanted to manufacture – which has nothing to do with consultancy and requires different skills. CCL took up 7.5% of the action and when Graham took Domino to the market in 1985, CCL realized £2.5 million, having originally invested some £50,000. They also take a royalty on the product sales.

This example shows a high tech spin-off, but they do not have to be high-tech. You might feel that the company you work for is ignoring certain markets that have potential. Your employer could be ignoring them for perfectly sound reasons – perhaps they are not central to the firm's activities or may be they are too small. This sort of dissatisfaction in you could be pointing at an opportunity for a sponsored spin-off. However you develop the idea, you will need to understand what benefits your employer could get from sponsoring your spin-off before you can make a reasonable job of selling the proposition to them.

There are many possible benefits for the sponsoring organization. These include firstly, taking advantage of new product developments. If you, as an employee, have a good idea for new product there is a possibility that you will want to keep the idea to yourself so as to be able to develop it on your own. If your employer has a policy of backing employees in such circumstances, if only with good advice, then you are far more likely to seek your employer's support, from which the company may profit.

Possible benefits may also be obtained through participating in profits from markets otherwise too small for the parent to consider exploitation. Here, companies which ignore openings in the market are inviting the more adventurous of its employers to set up on their own. The employees have the knowledge of the market place and if they spot an opportunity which the firm has neglected then, obviously, they will start thinking about ways in which to exploit the potential. If the parent has a policy of backing spin-offs it can participate in the profits generated in such a way.

The parent company may find that a spin-off policy can be a tremendous incentive to the management to think entrepreneurially, as it harnesses the entrepreneurial talent in the company.

You may also find that you can take advantage of opportunities which might otherwise have been left on the shelf. If Martin Brown had not decided to follow up the horse bandage business himself there would have been no convenient bandages at all.

You must be able to make the most use of the knowledge and skills which exist in the workforce.

All your efforts will, ultimately, help to diversify the parent's portfolio – many of the ideas which become spin-offs are related to, but not part of the main activities of the business, and hence allow diversification along rational lines. In fact, used properly, this can allow diversification along irrational lines – which could actually be very profitable. There is an argument which would have us believe, not too unreasonably, that major growth in companies comes from investing in areas which would never have been considered (by the company) some years earlier. This is especially true of industries where the rate of technological development is rapid. If this is true, then companies need some avenues which give them windows of opportunity on unthought of areas. Some people will have 'sky blue' ideas, from which, if their employer has a spin-off policy, the company can benefit.

That a small team of people who have autonomy can bring a product to market faster than a large firm can, with its committees and working groups, should prove a huge boon to a sponsoring company. It has been estimated that the speed differential commonly lies between nine and eighteen months. Being fast into a market improves the profit potential from that market.

A sponsored spin-off should improve the corporate image; the world at large and the financial press in particular still regard spin-offs as a 'good thing'. Added to which it should also help with recruitment. If a company has a spin-off policy it will find that it can attract good people more easily, since they will recognize the fact that their entrepreneurialism is more likely to be rewarded. Ultimately, too, the sponsoring company will inevitably benefit from the people who would have gone their own way anyway.

The sponsoring company can get all these benefits without losing focus on their mainstream activities:

> Alan Murphy, the marketing director of Cambridge Consultants, said, 'taking one's eye off the ball can be disastrous – protection of the core business is why we sponsor spin-offs.' CCL spin-offs have included Elmjet, launched 1986; Data Conversion, launched 1987; and they have now spun-off a venture capital company in which they have a quarter share, Prelude Technology Investments. As a consequence CCL no longer needs to take a share in spin-offs directly.

From your point of view, there are also many advantages; you will have a chance to make some capital gains, it gives you autonomy, and it can be a low risk entrance to owning your own business. Finally, having a corporate partner itself brings many benefits to a new venture such as management expertise, access to customers, and so on.

The Hive-Off

> Jane Stillwood worked for a medium-sized building contractor in Hitchin. The company decided that it would close the Hitchin office in favour of expanding its St Albans operation. Jane lived near the office and knew that her employer wanted an address in Hitchin for the company. She offered to administrate it and suggested that they let her have the office and its equipment, including her word processor and a facsimile machine. Using this she was then able to sell secretarial services back to her employer and to let part of the office on monthly licence.

Any company could sub-contract most parts of its business. In fact, many businesses start by doing just that. There are a variety of reasons why companies do not use sub-contracting more, which include control of quality, availability, company ethos, and most importantly, the cost.

Look around you in the department where you work. Can you identify a part which could be made into a separate company, selling a product or service back to the parent company. If you can, you may have found an opportunity for a hive-off.

The major factor is considering if a hive-off opportunity exists is whether or not the proposition can be made sufficiently attractive to the parent. You will have to overcome the big disadvantages of sub-contracting so far as the parent is concerned. Either that or persuade them that the cost saving you can produce for them will outweigh other considerations.

How to follow up

Following up a spin or hive off proposition is much like that of a buy-out. You probably need to start with a letter, subject to contract, to the managing director. However, there are some things you should do before going that far. There are also some factors you need to consider in advance of any offer from you, not least is how you will structure it.

The evaluation of the proposition should be done through the preparation and use of a business plan in the way suggested in the previous chapter.

In compiling it, consider that one study[1] suggests that to make a spin-off successful the sponsor must:

- allow separation from the rest of the organization;
- allow freedom to make long term decisions;
- not have tight control systems;
- give strong and clear support from senior management.

Consequently, your plan and its inherent proposal to the parent company should allow you these freedoms.

Where you need outside financial support you will have to take the business plan to a potential investor before going to the parent company. In this case you will have to consider the respective shareholdings you are willing to allow. In fact, you may not have any real control over that decision because you are going to be in the weakest position regarding any subsequent negotiations.

Investors In Industry (3i) prefer no-one to have voting control. An example of this situation is as follows:

---

1   Birley S., Manning K., Norburn D. *Implementing Corporate Venturing*, Working Paper Cranfield School of Management, 1987.

Microscribe Limited is a spin off from the Sector Group. The former manufactures miniature computers, amongst other things, and the latter works in computer design. Sector Group allowed the spin off and has retained 30% of the shares, so it now has a significant part of a business it would otherwise not have pursued. A venture capital company put in £175,000 of the £350,000 deal in return for 30% of the action and the management team have 40% between them.

Finally, the sponsoring company sometimes wants to have the right to buy in. They want an option to buy back the whole company at some later date, usually at fair valuation. I certainly would be the same in their shoes, as not to do so would exclude my company from some of the advantages outlined earlier in the chapter. Try not to let this happen too early, as it will have a stultifying effect on the company for a while after the event.

The aftermath

Peter Scott, the commercial manager of a high-tech company, recognized an opportunity for a fully sponsored spin-off from his company. He investigated the proposed business idea and found it very attractive. It had the added advantage of having benefits from his employers' point of view. He managed to convince the managing director that the spin-off would be advantageous for the parent company. The managing director suggested that it should be put before the full board. Peter prepared a super presentation for the board and sat back in full expectation of being showered with compliments and the permission to go ahead.

The research director stood up and, pointing at Peter said, 'it's him or me.' Since the research director founded the company and still had a majority shareholding, it was Peter – they fired him.

Entrepreneurship can misfire. Peter knew about the shareholding but had wrongly assumed that the managing director was the only one who needed persuading in advance. The company went on to put Peter's ideas into action without him.

In addition to all the above it is possible that companies do spin or hive off unwanted units. They probably do not do it as much as some companies would like because such a ringer would be spotted. But beware of suggestions coming from the sponsor rather than from an individual manager within the sponsor. It can be a way of disposing of unwanted employees.

As with buy-outs, great care is needed in everything involved in spin-offs.

Chapter Thirteen:
Filtering Ideas

Introduction

Once you have created ideas, you need to evaluate them to see if they are going to be beneficial for you. This evaluation can be looked at as a two stage process of researching the idea, then developing a plan for the launch and subsequent operation of the business.

The first is the subject matter of *Part III* of this book and the second is covered very well by existing books.

When you create ideas for potential businesses you are looking for the two or three 'best', 'strongest', 'most valuable' ideas, and so on. I put the words in inverted commas because the terms are subjective to you – what you would find good, strong or valuable is not necessarily what your neighbour would find good, strong, or valuable. You may be in the situation where you have created ten ideas or you might have created a thousand. However many or few ideas you currently have, you still have too many (I hope) to ask of each, Will it work? (See *Part III*.) You want to ask this question of as few ideas as possible, as it should be extremely time consuming.

> Linda Bennion wanted to start her own business but had no idea what to try. She set up a brainstorming session with some friends and ended up with 162 ideas. On their own, the ideas were useless to her. Which of the 162 should she do?
>
> As you can see, you need some sort of idea filter which is of sufficiently fine mesh to allow through only those two or three ideas strong enough to become businesses. This chapter shows how you can develop your own idea filter.

Immediate Action

Do absolutely nothing. It is best to wait a day or two before beginning the evaluation. Let things settle in your mind. There the ideas will stew for a while and you will be able to perform a more objective evaluation. And where you have generated a large number of ideas you also need to remember that for every good idea there will be ninety-nine bad ones – you are looking for the needle in the haystack.

Grouping Ideas

When you use techniques such as brainstorming or morphological analysis properly you are likely to end up with large numbers of ideas, many of which will be totally unsuitable. Many of them, too, will be reasonably similar to other ideas in the group. Using whatever criteria you like you could break the whole down into subsections of ideas with similar characteristics. Once you have done this you can evaluate the sub-group as a whole rather than as individual ideas and save yourself a lot of time.

> Linda was able to group the ideas into ones which related to work experience, advertising, training other people, art, retail, consultancy, off the wall, and other.
> Since her advertising work experience was what gave her the motivation to start her own business in the first place (she was tired of it), that group could go. She also felt that she did not have the right character to be a retailer, that group could go too. Consultancy did not offer the growth potential she wanted, so that was out. That left her with 59 ideas spread across the four categories: training other people; art; off the wall; and other.

Your Personal Framework

Earlier in the book you developed a framework derived from both what you want and what you would be happiest doing. Into that framework, you added the constraints on what you can do – little money, your desires for a social life, your inability to speak other languages, etc. You can now use this framework to help you filter the ideas you have generated.

How to use the framework

To be able to use the framework you add some numbers to your lists which rank the relative importance of the various objectives that you developed earlier. For example – is easiness more important to you than the lack of social life? Twice as important? If so then easiness will carry double the weight of any lack of social life. Does the promise of high profits rank higher than your desire to be in control of your own destiny, ie, autonomy? How much more important is it? Twice? Three times? How does the autonomy objective rank against the easiness objective?

Put some numbers against the objectives so as to be able to see their respective weight in their importance to you.

Linda's list of objectives and the associated weightings (their relative importance to her) were as follows:

Objective	Weight
autonomy	20
enjoyable	15
art related	10
challenge	9
meeting people	8
high profits	5
social life	5
holidays	3
high status	2

The next step is to add the constraints to the list and give them importance factors too.

Linda's were:

Constraint	Weight
must achieve minimum living wage	20
little money	10
experience	10
use home	10
employ daughter	5

For Linda, the proposed business' ability to produce a minimum living wage was as important as the autonomy that she desired so much.

The next step is to grade each idea against your objectives and constraints. Draw the table shown below for yourself, listing your objectives and constraints. Go through each idea and grade it against each category giving a score on the scale of 1 to 10.

As an example, four of Linda's 59 remaining ideas were to set up a private training college for trainees, an artists club where materials, tuition and studio space are available, bicycle tour agency, and a baby-sitting service.

These are the scores she gave them:

Fig. 1

OBJECTIVES AND CONSTRAINTS		IDEA							
		College		Artists Club		Bicycle Tours		Baby Sitting	
	weight	score	score × weight	score	score × weight	score	score × weight	score	score × weight
Autonomy	20	9		9		9		9	
Enjoyable	15	6		10		4		5	
Art Related	10	0		10		0		0	
Challenge	9	10		9		10		9	
People	8	9		9		8		7	
Profits	5	6		5		5		2	
Social Life	5	4		2		3		5	
Holidays	3	7		1		7		7	
Status	2	7		1		1		0	
Living Wage	20	9		7		8		4	
Money	10	1		9		9		10	
Experience	10	2		9		3		9	
Home	10	1		9		9		0	
Daughter	5	4		9		5		9	

The scores Linda gave the ideas were based on her perceptions of what was involved in that idea for that criterion. You must also score based on your own preferences and biases.

Before you go on to work out which idea is most attractive, add another line to your objectives and constraints – namely, your capabilities. Here you are trying to assess how well the idea matches your own character traits and capabilities. Because that is so important, I would give it a weight equal to that of your highest for any other.

Linda's grading against her capabilities has now been added to the table, as follows:

Fig. 2

OBJECTIVES AND CONSTRAINTS		IDEA							
		College		Artists Club		Bicycle Tours		Baby Sitting	
	weight	score	score × weight	score	score × weight	score	score × weight	score	score × weight
Autonomy	20	9		9		9		9	
Enjoyable	15	6		10		4		5	
Art Related	10	0		10		0		0	
Challenge	9	10		9		10		9	
People	8	9		9		8		7	
Profits	5	6		5		5		2	
Social Life	5	4		2		3		5	
Holidays	3	7		1		7		7	
Status	2	7		1		1		0	
Living Wage	20	9		7		8		4	
Money	10	1		9		9		10	
Experience	10	2		9		3		9	
Home	10	1		9		9		0	
Daughter	5	4		9		5		9	
Capabilities	20	7		9		5		3	

Finally, multiply the scores you gave each category by the associated weight, and add these figures up. The intention is that the idea which has the highest total ought to be the best idea so far as you are concerned. (*See fig. 3*).

Linda's scores are now shown in the following table:

Fig. 3

		IDEA							
OBJECTIVES AND CONSTRAINTS		College		Artists Club		Bicycle Tours		Baby Sitting	
	weight	score	score × weight	score	score × weight	score	score × weight	score	score × weight
Autonomy	20	9	180	9	180	9	180	9	180
Enjoyable	15	6	90	10	150	4	60	5	75
Art Related	10	0	—	10	100	0	—	0	—
Challenge	9	10	90	9	81	10	90	9	81
People	8	9	72	9	72	8	64	7	56
Profits	5	6	30	5	25	5	25	2	10
Social Life	5	4	20	2	10	3	15	5	25
Holidays	3	7	21	1	3	7	21	7	21
Status	2	7	14	1	2	1	2	0	—
Living Wage	20	9	180	7	140	8	160	4	80
Money	10	1	10	9	90	9	90	10	100
Experience	10	2	20	9	90	3	30	9	90
Home	10	1	10	9	90	9	90	0	—
Daughter	5	4	20	9	45	5	25	9	45
Capabilities	20	7	140	9	180	5	100	3	60
TOTAL			897		1258		952		823

For Linda, the ideas now have the following rank in terms of attractiveness to her; artists' club (total 1258), bicycle tours (total 952), baby-sitting (total 897), trainees' college (total 823).

Linda had to go through the other 55 ideas too – so it is not a short process – but I specifically included the idea which scored the most. She now has a business called Art Studio Venture in London, a year old at the time of writing, which is about to expand out of her first outlet – her home.

When you attempt this the first time you may well end up with things high on the list which, for some reason or another, you do not find as attractive as ones lower down the list. There are two reasons why this might happen. Firstly, many people find it hard to know explicitly what it is they like or dislike, so do not worry if you find yourself in this position. Examine why the lower ranked ones are more attractive to see if you can identify the criteria. Once you have done that you can go through the ideas again, this time scoring them on the additional criteria as well. Secondly, you have got the relative weightings wrong. Here again, you examine why the ideas are apparently misplaced to see if you can come to a better judgement on how important each of the criteria are.

Idea mapping

You might be happier using a pictorial evaluation rather than a numerical technique. In fact, it may well be worth using both: with numerical analysis you get one answer (the one with most points) which ignores the qualitative aspects of the evaluation. Also with numerical analysis you do not get the benefit of comparing one idea with another. It is possible to map the ideas on a grid, allowing you to evaluate the ideas from where they lie on the grid. Thus you get an at-a-glance technique.

It takes a little longer to compile than at-a-glance would imply.

 (i) number the ideas on your list (writing up the list first, if you have not already done so.
 (ii) get some graph paper and draw a box ten units wide by ten units deep:
 (iii) across the top write 'objectives'; down the side write 'constraints'.
 (iv) add a ten point scale, (see *fig. 4*).

Go through the ideas one by one and grade each with two numbers between one and ten. The first grade should be how well the idea fits in with the objectives you developed as a result of the plan in Part I. If you have followed the advice earlier and ranked your ideas already, this grading is made easier since it is really the sum of the gradings you gave then. The second grade is how well, overall, the idea fits in with your constraints, taking into account your capabilities.

Suppose that Linda's four ideas were graded as follows:

	objectives score	constraints score
1. artists' club	9	7
2. bicycle tours	6	8
3. baby-sitting	4	9
4. trainees' college	5	3

then she could place each idea's number in the box, so:

Fig. 4

Fig. 4 — Grid: OBJECTIVES (columns 10 to 1) against CONSTRAINTS (rows 10 to 1). Idea 3 at objectives 4, constraints 9; idea 2 at objectives 6, constraints 8; idea 1 at objectives 9, constraints 7; idea 4 at objectives 5, constraints 3.

Using this system, the closer an idea is to the top left hand corner, the more attractive it is to you. In Linda's case, the artists' club probably still wins, but at least now she can make a qualitative judgement about the relative merits of the ideas. Where you have a large number of ideas to filter, you may find it best to eliminate as many as possible using the numerical analysis and then apply idea mapping to those which remain.

How?

By asking yourself, 'How do I put this idea into action?' you get an excellent mechanism for evaluating each idea's practicality. Many ideas are simply too impractical to implement, and thus you will not want to spend much time over them.

Try to work out what steps are involved in operationalizing this idea. Are they too impractical to achieve? Each step that you identify will have different parts or stages in it. Are these too impractical to achieve?

PART III: WILL IT WORK?

You now have an idea or, hopefully, several. What happens next? You cannot simply take your idea and turn it into a business overnight, there is much work to be done on the idea first.

Having got this far in the book at least we can be assured that any ideas you have generated fit in with your own personal objectives. Hopefully, too, they fit in with your strengths and weaknesses, needing more of the first and little of the second.

Of themselves, ideas do not achieve objectives – you need to do several things before launching your business including researching the idea properly, then plan for launch and subsequent operation.

There are lots of books and even training courses to help you plan and launch your business. So this part of the book helps you check out whether an idea is worth pursuing. In other words, it should help you answer the question, 'Is it worth bothering to plan for the launch and subsequent operation of this particular business idea?' It does this by asking first 'Why will people pay for my product/service?' Secondly, it looks at markets and what you need to know about a market for your idea. Finally, it includes a chapter of suggestions about where to find detailed answers to some of the questions you will be asking yourself.

Chapter Fourteen:
Why Will People Pay?

If an idea is going to be successful as a business someone is going to have to pay money for the final product or service offered. If you can answer, 'Yes' to the question, 'Will people pay?' then you probably have an idea that is beginning to look reasonable in business terms. Understanding why people pay for the things will help you answer whether people will pay for the product or service idea you want to look at.

First you need to understand the customers in terms of the benefits they can offer you.

Benefits

This is pretty fundamental to any business and getting this wrong means you will not be getting the right message across to your customer. Indeed, your idea will flounder at this stage if your understanding of the benefits (as opposed to features) is low:

> Lloyd Milsom was planning to start a West Indian Bakery in South East London. He and his partners stood outside the premises they planned to sell from and asked people if they currently ate the ethnic products that Lloyd was planning to sell. Sufficiently large numbers of people said yes for Lloyd to continue planning his launch with a splash using the message 'Come To Us: We Are Better!' (ie, better than the other four traditional bakers in the same High Street). His prospective customers stayed away in droves. Only after he changed his message to 'Buy From Us and Save Time!' did he get a thriving business.
>
> What Lloyd had not realized was that the people who were saying yes to his questions could not have been buying the West Indian product in that street because the other (traditional) bakers did not sell it. He came to the realization that they (his prospective cus-

tomers) must have been baking at home. No one who enjoys home cooking will buy a product which insults their cooking by proclaiming that 'We Are Better' (than you, customer).

Spotting the benefits from the features is not as easy as it sounds. So when you are given a cheap mug with New York on the side you will understand that the giver does not think that you cannot afford your own crockery (the feature). Rather he or she is trying to tell you that he or she is both the sort of person who goes to New York, and the sort of friend, even with all the distractions that New York has to offer, cares sufficiently strongly about you to buy you a gift (the benefits).

Try the Wheel Test on your idea. For a car to fulfil its function it has to have a wheel at each corner but do the buyers of cars find that important? Of course not, they are far more interested in whether a car's wheels have whitewall tyres. So that the fact that the wheel should be round is remarkable only when it is not round, and I will not pay you for roundness in wheel. But give it white wall tyres and it becomes a tool of the eternal struggle for me to 'look better' than you, and I will pay a fortune for that.

Essentially, marketing a product or service is all about matching your idea's capabilities with the needs of the market place.

Understanding the customer

There are a number of things of which you need to have a general understanding in order to operate in a market place. As we saw from the previous section customers have needs and wants, and you need also to understand that your customer is not necessarily going to be the same as your consumer. Let us suppose that you have decided that your idea is to manufacture a new type of soft drink. If this is the case, it will be the wholesalers and retailers who are your customers, as you will be selling to them. Their customers are likely to become your consumers, but even then might be one further removed because it might be the parent which buys the product for consumption by a child.

> Nick started a business manufacturing childrens' beds. The product was well designed and very attractive. The beds became trains or fire engines.
>
> Nick came to the market with a product idea but without having looked at the market place – he knew nothing of whether there was a need for such beds and even less of how to get them to the end buyer.

He found customer resistance because the people to whom he tried to sell the bed, were not the sort of people who would buy a bed whose design limited its use to a couple of years. There are people who will pay to change their kids' rooms as they grow older, but Nick did not find the right channels to reach them.

In all of these cases you have to find out what motivates the customer to buy from you.

Your product needs to have a number of attributes. It needs at least one unique trait, and your promotional message must be aimed at the right market or through suitable channels. Often you will not be selling direct to the customer so your product needs to have some benefits for the person who stocks it; that would then increase their sales because it would sell faster than other soft drinks lines.

If you remember that well in excess of 90% of all aftershave is bought by women for men, then you can apply this same principle to your own business idea. Make sure, therefore, that you have a market.

The second fundamental factor is called the adoption process and concerns the speed at which customers buy a product or service for the first time.

Do you remember cocktails? Courage does! The cocktail had been just about forgotten as a drink until the early nineteen eighties, when cocktail bars such as Rumours in Covent Garden began to open, catering for a very few fashionable innovators. Rumours was the in-place. To be seen there was to know (in your own eyes at least) that you were a fashion leader. An article in a Sunday colour supplement led to Rumours needing doormen as large numbers came to see and be seen. People continued to come in waves, rubber-necking all the time. After a time the place stopped being jam-packed and became just packed. Then just busy. Then it did not need doormen. Eventually a re-launch or closure. This is the adoption process.

How much of your market place does each segment take? The innovators are two and a half per cent of the total and the others are as follows:

- early adopters: 13½%
- early majority: 34%
- late majority: 34%
- laggards: 16%

We can illustrate it graphically as follows:

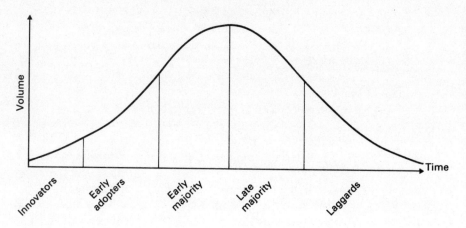

The Product/Service Adoption Process

You can be reasonably certain that you will not be able to sell to the early adopter type until the innovators have bought. The early majority need to see the early adopters using the product or service before they will, and the late majority need to see the early majority . . . and so on.

This has a fundamental implication for anyone starting a business, and that is, that any new business faces its own adoption curve. No matter what, the product has to offer something to tempt the customers away from their existing source of supply ('a unique selling point', of which, more later). If it does, a few might change and tell their friends who also might come and – and soon you have the adoption process.

All of this is especially true for restaurants, night clubs, bars, discos or any thing which has a 'fashion' tag to it. In these cases the adoption process can be extremely short. You can still make money in such circumstances and lots of it, but the astute bar owner is the one with his eye on what comes next.

As if that were not enough, each product or service has its own adoption process which we call the product life-cycle.

Product life-cycle

The product life-cycle looks much like the adoption curve as follows:

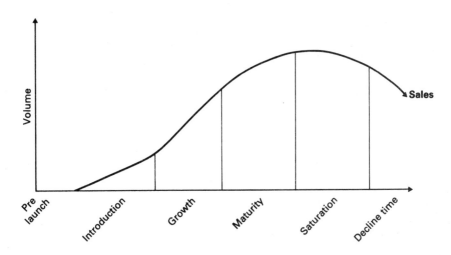

Fig. 1

If you graph sales volume against time it will have a curve much like that shown in the graph. Any new business idea has a period from the point at which the idea is generated, (now) to the point at which it achieves first sales, which we call the pre-launch period, where there are no sales at all. Then there is an introduction period when sales start coming in a slow manner. Here you start making initial sales but there are no repeat sales yet, and new customers are still coming – but slowly. Towards the end of this period you are beginning to sell more – things are beginning to look encouraging. You get one or two repeat sales and you go on to the next section which is sales growth. Here the business is really becoming established, customers are referring new customers to you and also buying more themselves. Your new sales are quite high and your repeat sales are growing fast. The speed at which your sales turnover increases is usually phenomenal at this point.

This period is followed by one of maturity where the speed of growth in sales volume slows down slightly. The customers have become aware of the product. They no longer find it new and the excitement in the market place is beginning to be replaced by one of contented satisfaction knowing that the product is valued by one's customers. During the mature phase sales are still increasing but during the saturation phase they may not be. Here you have just about gone as far as you are going to go with that particular product you have reached a market share and there are no new customers coming into the market place. Growth in the market place has stopped. Finally, decline must follow. Here the customers are moving on to other products and other market places, leaving yours behind. The product has become less fashionable and there are substitutes available.

It is easier to make money with a product that's in the growth, the mature stage or even the saturation stage than it is with one that's in the decline. However that does not mean it is not perfectly possible to make a lot of money with products in the decline stage.

Knowing where your business is on the life-cycle is a very important, not least because its position will determine how you phrase your promotional messages. Another major consideration, perfected by where you are on the product life-cycle, will be your competitive strategy. If the market place is declining then everybody will be fighting for a smaller pool of customers, causing price wars and other cut throat competitive factors. If people are competing in a growing market place then everybody's sales are likely to be increasing as new customers come into that market place and there will be less ferocious competition. People will need to make reductions in their margins by reducing their prices in such areas.

Let us look first at the difference in the promotional messages in different places on the product life-cycles. For anyone to buy anything at all from you three things must first happen:

- The public must be made aware of you and your product; so if you do build a better mouse trap the world will not beat a path to your door without your first making it aware.
- They must be interested enough to investigate whether or not to buy it, and you must make them aware not only of the mousetrap but also of the fact that it is better than other mousetraps.
- They must decide to buy your product, and you must make them aware that your mousetrap is better value for money or more efficient than their existing supplies.

This is important because, if your product is in the early stages you first have to make your customer aware of the product and this can be difficult, time consuming and costly. For example:

> Guy Maidwell runs a CD outlet in London. When he first opened, he was having to spend most of his time explaining what CD stood for, that they were worked using lasers, and that they were digitally recorded, before he could make a sale. Nowadays, he need only

discuss the merits of one system over another saving him and his sales people a lot of time (and therefore, saving him money).

To summarize, if your new product is in the earlier part of its life-cycle you will have a costly educational component to add to your sales promotion, instead of being able to say, 'buy our product because we try harder.'

Life-cycles differ quite significantly in terms of time. Think of a party:

> For a fee Finches, run by Tessa Finch, will organize you a party or ball. All the hard work will be done in pre-planning the party and actually most shifting and back breaking work is done in the twenty-four hours leading up to the start time of 8.00 pm (the pre-launch effort). Between 8.00 and 8.30 pm you start panicking because only one person has turned up (first sale), and that is someone you dislike. Between 8.30 and 9.00 pm you relax as four more couples turn up (early sales). Between 9.00 and 10.00 pm you never get away from the door as people are arriving all the time (growth/maturity). Between 10.00 and midnight very few people turn up (saturation), and everybody is having a good time. Between midnight and 1.00 am a small number of people leave (saturation/early decline). Between 1.00 and 2.00 am you, again, never leave the door (decline) and between 3.00 and 4.00 am you are actively suggesting to the few die-hards left that they leave.
>
> Tessa's parties have life-cycles of only hours but the life-cycle for Tessa's service can be counted in decades or even centuries.

So, is the idea you are currently looking at early or late in the product life-cycle terms? The easiest place to be selling is in a market showing fast growth just prior to maturity and/or a recently matured marketplace.

Having defined where the idea is on its own product life-cycle turn back to the problem that your idea, if turned into a business, will face during its own adoption process. How will you get the innovators to buy your product or service? What will tempt them away from the existing sources of supply? Is there anything unique about what you are planning to do? Because, if there is not, you may as well drop the idea out at this stage.

Originality

Why should people bother coming to you for their goods and services rather than to Fred Bloggs down the road? What is so special about you? Where the answer is nothing there is no business; customers do need some difference, something unique in an idea, business or product/service before they will change the source of supply they already use.

There are a lot of reasons why people should not change. Initially, they will not know you personally, so why should they listen what you have to say? They may have built up a track record or relationship with their existing supplier. They also know what they already buy from their existing supplier works for them.

This list of reasons could go on much, much longer. You have to be able to create a difference of sufficient value to the customer, so that it overcomes the natural inertia inherent in people in general, and in customers in particular. We call the difference a unique selling point (USP). USPs are vital to any business idea.

In the following example I have changed the name of the individual but not the facts of his story.

> George Harris wanted to set up a nursing agency in South East London, providing trained staff, other than doctors, to local hospitals to cover short term needs. There were already four such agencies operating. He took this as a good sign; that if there were already four there must be a market and room for one more. He opened his doors for business and attracted a number of nurses to his books. He did not make a single sale and closed his doors poorer, but hopefully wiser, four months later.

George's major problem was that he had absolutely no USPs. When he went selling he could not argue that his nurses were better quality because to a large extent they were the same nurses as on the other agencies' books. He might have been able to offer better service in administration terms but is that valued by his customers who need nurses? Who was George Harris anyway? An ex-NHS employee, and he had no special or unique services to offer. He made no sales either.

Uniqueness, in the sense of USPs, is not necessarily inventing a machine, or similar. The originality could rest on something as simple as the location of your business idea. A really good USP is quality. Can you build a better quality product or service into your idea? If you can, you could end up with a really successful business because you will be able to charge more than anyone else.

Other USPs can be created through more convenience, time-saving, appealing to vanity, longer lasting, money saving, fashion, younger looking, fitter, more comfort, envy, more profit, faster selling, making/building faster, needing fewer employees, or easier selling.

If you can create USPs or if your business idea has USPs which have some of the above attributes you will probably have an idea which is worth exploring further. If you can compete on such things – you might even be able to charge more than your competition because people will value what you have to sell. Your competitors will find it difficult to imitate your USPs (or they would not be unique) and thus find it hard to compete in those areas.

Nowhere in the above has price been mentioned. How could price be ignored? Cheap prices are rotten USPs for a new business. They are not unique because anyone can do it. Your competition in the marketplace where you propose to take this idea could probably wipe you out on price in a very short time.

> George Harris, (of the nursing agency), had decided that he would be able to compete in the market because he would be cheaper by, on average, one pound per hour of labour supplied, than his competitors. When he went to sell to the hospitals he found a lot of interest but no one bought. Soon he found his four competitors had lowered their prices to his level. He cut his prices and went back to the hospitals. Again he found much interest but no sales. Soon his four competitors had cut their prices to his level.
>
> The lesson George learned from this whole process that as a USP, price can be wiped out at the drop of a hat.

In the example it looked as though George's competitors were ganging up on him in a concerted fashion. This proved not to be true – George was bringing it all on himself. Trying to compete on price for George was simply suicidal. Not only that, but it would have had a murderous effect on the whole marketplace for a period of time.

Finally, you should have some idea now how to match your idea against some of the things a customer needs and buys. You now need to be able to judge whether or not an idea is worth exploring and to do this you need to look a little further. Look into the market for the idea itself.

Chapter Fifteen:
Who Will Buy?

Your Idea's Market Place

Before you can judge whether or not to take the first active steps in commercializing any idea you are going to need knowledge regarding your business' market place in particular and about market places in general. You not only need to know why people buy but also which particular people will buy your product. In addition you need to know what avenues, tools and techniques will be available to you when you start to sell your idea.

This chapter will also help you determine your information requirements: 'What do I need to know to be able to assess whether this idea is worth pursuing?'

First we will look at segments.

Segments

If you have an idea for a product or service, you must ask, who will you be selling to, if you get this idea off the ground? There are only three alternatives; businesses, non profit making organizations, or people as people (rather than as representatives of organizations).

You have already seen that to make sales your idea must be capable of producing benefits; your product or service must have something which helps your customers achieve their own objectives in some way better than other suppliers. It must have USP's. These USP's will only be of value in certain areas or to specific people. Something that is of value to us as individuals cannot be of value to a business or other organization except in so far as it wants to sell on or give it to us. So each of our three alternatives have different methods of valuing a product or service which is being offered.

All of our three categories value a product or service that they are being offered by reference to their own objectives, whether consciously or un-consciously. Hence, if your idea involves customers which are businesses, your new concept's USP's should help generate more profit for them. This group of potential customers are reasonably similar in their objectives.

Similarly, non profit making organizations very often have common objectives of providing their services more effectively and at a reduced cost.

Again, this group of potential customers are reasonably similar in their objectives.

However, the third group, 'people as people', differ very widely. You are unique, aren't you? So understanding what drives us to buy any product or service is very difficult. As a group and taken as a whole, we the people, show very few common characteristics. As a result, we the people, taken as a whole, are extremely difficult to sell to. You will have to sell to bits of us. For example, is the following promotional message going to appeal to a seventy-five year old?:

> Come on our sailing holiday where our beach parties
> can last through the night.

These different bits of us are called segments. It is a whole lot easier understanding what a particular segment may value. Consequently any idea where the potential customer can be segmented by common characteristics is much more likely to be worth pursuing than one of which this cannot be said.

There are a number of factors you need to take into account when trying to identify if a segment exists and where your idea might thrive.

> Chantal Coady runs Rococo, a shop on the Kings Road, Chelsea, selling high quality, hand made chocolates at extremely high prices. Chantal now has her segmentation worked out perfectly well. Before the opening she defined her potential customers as the 'general public'.

Let me tell you, that firstly, a very large chunk of the population of London, let alone of the population of Great Britain (our general public) goes nowhere near the Kings Road, Chelsea. Secondly, a very large proportion of the population does not buy chocolates, and thirdly, a very large chunk of the population does not buy chocolates which cost in excess of £8 per pound.

The point is that your segments must be sufficiently small that they have some common characteristics. In Chantal's case some of the common characteristics were a willingness to shop in the Kings Road, the desire to buy chocolates, and a fair degree of wealth.

So your idea needs a segment or segments which are sufficiently small to have identifiable common characteristics but also large enough for your idea to thrive.

One last thing about your idea's potential segments is that you must be able to communicate with them at reasonable cost.

> A company called Blooming Marvellous sells clothes to the mother-to-be who wants to be fashionably dressed.
>
> Blooming Marvellous have segmented their market place very well; female, aged mostly between 16 and 40, fashion conscious, and pregnant.

Not only have they identified their segment well but they are able to communicate with it easily through the mother and baby magazines which proliferate today.

So, if your idea is worthwhile, you should be able to describe a model or ideal customer. What motivates them, what gender, where they live, how old they are, how many children they have, and so on. More importantly, you should be able to say why this particular segment will value the end product of your idea sufficiently well to move from their existing suppliers to you.

Finally if you can identify the first customers, preferably by name, and state why they, in particular, will buy your product when it comes to market then you probably have an excellent idea from which to start planning.

Competition

Most people regard the existence of other firms selling products and services similar to their own as a bad thing. However, most companies chase bigger and bigger shares of their specific market places.

> Dominic and Sarah own and run Café Bistro near Greenwich in South East London. Whilst talking about their business one day Dominic said that a new restaurant was opening up three doors away. In the traditionalists' eyes, Dominic should have been tearing his hair out. He was however extremely happy – two restaurants together mean more and in particular help create longer lasting trade than either could generate on their own.

Having competition can, therefore, be excellent news.

Where would you set up an antiques outlet in London? Either the Portobello Road or Bond Street, depending on the quality of the antiques. Because that is where everyone else is.

> Justin Watch is planning to launch a successor to a puzzle called the Dragon Lock. He is planning the launch for the Spring of 1989 when the Dragon Lock will be three years old.

Justin is planning to use the competition's effort to make people aware of his product. This can be absolutely vital to any business idea. Justin timed his launch to save himself a lot of marketing effort (and thus a lot of marketing costs). For Justin, the absence of competition would be disastrous.

Having competition who are willing to make both their own and, as a result, your customer aware, can be a great boon, especially for ideas which rely on new market places or technologies. The absence of competition, usually in the form of a bigger firm willing to do this, can really slow your idea down.

Graham Kentsley runs Telstar, a firm selling satellite TV systems. Everyone in satellite TV knows that the market is going to 'take off' in a big way soon. However no-one is willing to take on board the massive awareness campaigns that remain necessary to educate a potential consumer market. This is slowing everyone down, including Graham, and everyone is competing for a relatively small number of aware customers.

This example brings out two points regarding competition for an idea. The first is that if an idea you have generated already has competition this should be regarded as an encouraging sign. They will have been the trail blazers making people aware of your product's existence. You can use their marketing efforts, especially advertising, to help your own.

Remember the man who was 'so impressed with the electric shaver that he bought the company?'. BIC razors now have a poster campaign for their disposable razors which reads, 'I was so impressed I bought the bag'.

The latter, which gets messages across really well, would have been impossible without the first slogan.

The second factor, that the Kentsley example brings out, is that competing in a currently very slowly growing market (as in Graham's case) or competing in static and declining market places is usually completely different to competing in a growing market.

Imagine your market place as being a large circle:

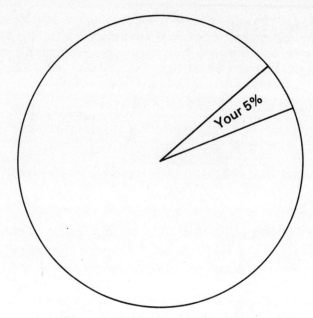

Figure 1: The Market and Your Share.

You have five per cent of the market and you are happy. Suppose the whole market place grows rapidly over the next year so that it becomes as follows:

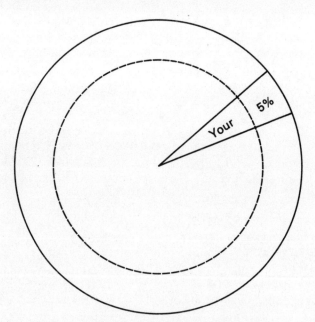

Figure 2: The Enlarged Market and Your Share.

172

If you manage to retain as much as five per cent of the whole you would be ecstatic since your turnover would have more than doubled. At the same time, every other company supplying that market (your competition) is experiencing similar growth in sales. You are not having to fight each other to help your sales grow.

Suppose your market place were declining, as follows:

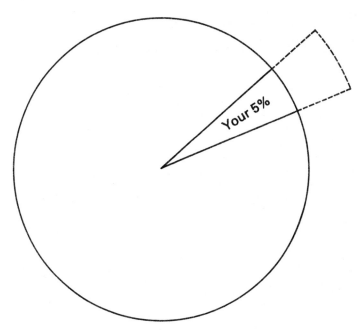

Figure 3: The Reduced Market Place and Your Share

If you still only keep with five per cent of the market, your sales will fall in proportion to the decline in the market. If you want your sales to increase in these circumstances you have to increase your market share.

It sounds simple enough. But what you tend to forget is that if you manage to increase your sales volume by one per cent in a declining market you have taken more than one per cent away from a competitor. In a declining market, your growth is therefore at your competitors' cost.

They may even regard that as a type of theft and respond accordingly. There will be price wars, attacks on your product's previously good reputation and all sorts of cut-throat competition. Your margins and profits will be under severe pressure. You will have major headaches.

Many firms consider increased market shares as the be all and end all of competitive strategy. But an increase in market share for one is a reduction in market share for another, and inevitably, the opposition will put pressure on your profits. Personally, I would far rather try to get increases in turnover from encouraging the whole market to grow thus retaining the high margins that good profitability needs.

So far this chapter should have prompted you to ask whether there is a segment (a market place) for the product or service? and whether it is increasing or declining in size? A third vital question you must address is 'How big is the segment in total?' That is to say – if you were to get one hundred per cent of the market place for your product or service how much would your sales revenue be?

It is important to know, because if your idea needs fifty per cent of the total to be able to make profits, then your idea is not very commercial. If you are IBM you might just be able to achieve fifty per cent of a market place, but most of us must be content with much smaller figures.

In fact, the smaller the better. I would be far happier for you if your idea needs only fifty per cent of one per cent of one per cent (or 1/200th of one per cent) of the total market for it to thrive because this is a far more realistic target, in the initial stages, than anything over one per cent.

So, to the questions you are asking of your idea you can add another; 'How big is the segment I am hoping to aim for with the idea?'

Marketing tools

When anyone takes a new product or service to a market it has four tools to help it sell under its control. These are the product, the place, the price, and the promotion. Marketing people call them the four P's or the Marketing Mix.

Why do you need to know about marketing tools now? Now, when you are only just at the stage of whether or not an idea is likely to be worth commercialising? Let me answer that by quickly running through all four.

The product or service on offer must be made to fit in with what the customer needs. When investigating your business idea, you have to ask what your customer will value about your product or service. Will it be the packaging or the colour that makes them more beautiful or handsome?

The place refers to where you actually make your product or service available. Where does your segment expect it to be? It has been said that the three most important factors in the success of any business are location, location, and location!

> Karl Gibbons, the founder of Flash Trash, has a location policy which places his shops within two hundred yards of Marks and Spencer, preferably on the same street.

When your customers are coming to you to buy, rather than you taking your product or service to them, location is vital. So where do your potential customers expect to buy their supplies?

Price is extremely important to any business. You must know whether or not you would command sufficiently high prices should you ever launch your idea. 'Can I get the margins I need to have a profitable business?'

Promotion, here, refers to any communication between you and your market with the intention of promoting more sales. It includes advertising, personal selling, public relations or anything designed to get your promotional messages across. Here, you need to know how the market for your idea learns of the products available, and how interest is generated.

Conclusion

We have laid out some of the more important factors about a potential market place for your idea. When looking at the idea further, you need to concentrate on finding answers to the following questions which are only the more important ones:

- Is there a segment for your idea's product/service?
- Is it growing?
- How big is it?
- What does it expect of and value in your product/service?
- Where would it like your product/service to be located?
- At what price? and,
- What promotional messages and media work are persuading this segment?

How to get the answers becomes apparent in the next chapter.

Chapter Sixteen:
Investigating

Introduction

Wellington, arguably our greatest military strategist, has said of reconnaissance that it is 'to endeavour to find out what you don't know from what you do . . . guessing what is at the other side of the hill'.

Market Research is your equivalent of Wellington's reconnaissance. It helps you investigate an idea for its commerciality. It helps you to decide whether or not to pursue the idea or to go to the trouble of raising finance, finding premises and launching your product.

Like most people who think about starting a business you are coming to your market place with a product – or service-related idea, rather than a market-based idea. This means that you know a lot about your idea and little about your potential market.

Market Research is the most important tool that you can use in looking at any business idea. Doing some Market Research is like taking out insurance, in that it does not achieve any of your objectives directly but it could save you a lot of time and money.

Ian Kent set up a magazine as a freebie in his local area. His idea was that his magazine, a high quality product, would be read more than the free local newspapers, giving any advertiser the benefit of knowing that his advertising would be more effective in that it would be reaching more people. Ian set the business up without doing any market research at all. He originally planned to make it a quarterly magazine. During the selling process necessary in getting the first issue off the ground, some customers suggested that it would be better if the mag were to be monthly. Ian was swayed by this and told his customers that the magazine would be monthly instead. He was having to rely on other companies for his typesetting and printing, and could find no-one who could help him fulfil his 'monthly' promise. As a result Ian had to go back, cap in hand, to the people who had booked and paid for space to ask them to advertise in his 'bi-monthly' magazine. Is it likely that you would have been interested in spending your scarce money with Ian after he had proved so unreliable? Ian never got enough advertising to get the second issue off the ground.

There is no doubt that Ian's idea was a perfectly good one. Certainly it was one worth spending time on. The problems which forced him to call it a day had their roots in his unreliability. He had employed typesetters and printers whose production schedules could handle quarterly issues without problems. Once he decided to alter the production schedule, he was obliged to use different suppliers whose approach to production was on a different time-scale. Ian is now £30,000 poorer, and he will have to forfeit his home.

Ian could easily have invested in some market research to discover whether monthly, bi-monthly or quarterly issues would have been best, long before he ever committed a penny to the launch of the idea.

You do not have hire other companies to do it for you either. It does not have to be expensive. He needed to establish a clearer idea of what would have attracted his potential customers and how often they wanted to see the magazine come out. He would also have benefited from having clearer information objectives.

Having clear objectives for what you need to know is vital in the process. If you do not really know what questions you are trying to answer you will end up with lots of interesting information, of which little can be usefully used. Sit down and ask yourself what you need to know before rushing off to talk to all those friends.

The suggestions given earlier will help you decide what to aim for, but what can you reasonably expect to get, in information terms?

Important Knowledge

This section will look first at general areas that need attention in ascertaining whether an idea is viable. Secondly, it will structure the information so that you will be able to get the best use from it.

Market Research can answer questions in two basic areas, about the market place itself, and it can discover what causes the customer in your market to buy any products in general, or different products in particular.

To begin, you will need an understanding of what factors are of particular importance to your business idea, and you will need to investigate the three main characteristics of your market place, namely, size, customers, and competition.

In terms of size you need to know how many, how often, and how much;

- how many customers there are,
- how often they buy (ie, the volume of sales), and
- how much they pay each time they buy (the value of sales).

What you are interested in is what your future expectations, rather than what is happening now or happened in the past. However, all the information you can reliably collect, details the past track record. Consequently you will have to use that to see if you can identify future trends.

You will need to have some understanding of your customers. The segments that might suit your idea will have identifiable characteristics (if there are no identifiable characteristics there may not be sufficient customers to make a market of them). What are these characteristics? Who will buy the product? Can you identify reasons why some people buy more than others?

Your prospective competitors can prove to be a mine of useful information. They have been around the market place for some while now and consequently must have understood their customers, and offered what was required.

What are the factors in their success? They could be worth imitating if your planned business has the same criterion, and particularly if they have some established strengths in your prospective market place. You need to know what these are, because to compete with a company on its own strengths is often a recipe for disaster. Your competition will also have weaknesses in the market place, and knowing where these lie, lets you develop a competitive edge for your idea.

One might classify the above as 'market' data because the market is being outlined. You also need data on what is important to the customer in terms of how you can change the way he or she currently spends money, because if your idea is to succeed you have to persuade them to move their custom to you. You could call this approach 'marketing' data – what you are trying to establish is what influences change in your idea's market.

You need to know the what, why, where, when, and how of the market. For example;

- What price?
- Why is it bought?
- Where is it bought?
- When it is bought?
- How does the customer learn of it?
- How is it bought?

Who Should Do The Research?

Most people think of market research as something for which you have to hire professionals – companies may charge as much as £1,200 per day and you probably cannot afford such sums at this stage.

Do it yourself. After all, to begin with you are only attempting to find out whether there is a sufficiently large market out there. If the research shows that the market stands at around £100 million and you only need to get a turnover of £100,000 then it is irrelevant if your market size data is out by a factor of 100 per cent but it shows that your idea is probably workable.

How to get the answers

The best way to get answers of any kind is from people who have asked similar questions or researched similar areas themselves. Quite often you will find that you do not have to reinvent the wheel – you would be amazed at the amount of publicly available information. Finding out anything from previously published information is called Desk Research.

Desk research

Desk research has the benefit of taking less effort than the other main source of information – asking people, or field research. Field researchers are often on the streets talking to passers by, although your idea might involve only talking to people down the phone. You will probably have to do some of both sorts if you are to check your idea thoroughly, which you must.

Desk Research has two major advantages over field research: it is easier (since the information is already available) and it is cheaper (especially in terms of your time). It is also a good indication of things such as a rough total market size.

> When Sue Claridge was planning to start her restaurant she was able to find (from government statistics) that there was a population of 120,000 people in the town where she planned to set up. Twenty-seven per cent were between twenty and thirty years old (which was her segment) and for the group of people there was an average of £4.70 spent, per head, per week, on eating out. Hence her total market was estimated at £4.70 × 120,000 × 27% × 52 each year. That is to say, their target segment was spending in the

region of £8 million (7,918,560) on eating out each year. Her first year's turnover was expected to be £160,000 and, therefore, they needed to achieve two per cent of the total market, a reasonable target given the amount of competition in the town concerned.

Desk research also has a major drawback when compared to field research in that it may be less relevant to your business idea. Desk research depends on already published sources for its information, ie, someone else's field research. By its very nature it is out of date and you have no idea of its current worth. In Sue Claridge's case the £4.70 was a figure for the country as a whole and hence wrong for her area.

So a combination of both Desk and Field research will be necessary. Firstly, you should find out where to get published information. There are three major sources, your own records, Governmental publications, and Non-governmental publications, of which your own records are the most reliable and the most useful. Obviously, at this stage this most reliable of sources is not available to you as you have not yet set up. You do not yet have the customer sales, costs, and profits records and all the data which an established business has. However, most people in business forget that their existing operations are the best place to start if they are looking for information regarding how to expand current sales or launch new products.

The Government collects and publishes all sorts of information and statistics which are useful to anyone investigating their idea. The Central Office of Information produces much of the data. It has the advantage of being conducted among large numbers of people and firms and can therefore be considered as reasonably reliable. However, the information is also often too wide ranging and out of date.

Non-governmental sources might include newspapers, reference books, trade associations produced data, databanks, universities and research associations. All of those could have important information, useful to anyone looking at an idea for a business.

A guide to sources of information is reproduced in Appendix I. Libraries and Librarians are both useful and normally very helpful for prospective business people.

Field research

Field research tends to be far more time consuming than desk research since you have all sorts of things to do before you can collect the data. It is certainly more costly than desk research – you will have transport costs, stationery costs, and telephone costs, at the least.

In a statistical sense, the data collected will be less reliable than the data published in, say, the Central Statistical Office's reports. This is because you will be collecting information from a relatively small sample of people. However, this disadvantage could well be outweighed by the greater relevance to yourself of the data you collect. Hopefully, you will be getting information from the very people who may become your customers.

> Sue Claridge stood on the street outside her prospective premises and asked passers-by what they spent on going to restaurants each week on average. It turned out her target segment spent £10 per week. She was therefore able to get a more relevant (although possibly less reliable) assessment of her total market at £16.8 million.

Sue's questions were a lot more targeted than appears in the above example, as they would have to be if the information gained is to be of any use.

Data can be collected in the field by two basic methods, simply using your eyes or asking people. The first is observation;

> George Duckett wanted to open a print gallery. He had been offered a shop on a secondary shopping street close to the town centre. He sat in the café across the street for eight separate hours (week-day lunch, Saturday morning, late week-day evening, etc.) to count the foot traffic flow outside the shop.

This helped George tremendously since he had earlier collected some data on an apparently successful outlet in another town. There he counted the foot traffic flow at various times. He was also able to collect data on how many came out with a purchase. Since he knew (through earlier observation) what their price ranges were, he was able to estimate their turnover. Because he could now estimate what percentage of passers-by entered the shop and subsequently bought something he got a good idea of the attractiveness of the property he had been offered.

To make George's data more reliable, he should have repeated it, not only for several weeks but also in different seasons, summer/winter, etc. Naturally, you will have to sacrifice some reliability for speed. You must ask enough people to make the results reliable as a guide to whether or not to pursue the idea in its current form, but not asking so many as to make the task beyond your resources.

As a guideline let me suggest that your own circle of friends and aquaintances is probably not enough. They will probably be biased in favour of you and therefore the information you get from them will be highly unreliable. Somewhere between fifty and 200 people is usually an adequate sample.

Asking people for information can be structured in a variety of ways. The two extremes are as an unstructured chat or a formal questionnaire with no open questions. The unstructured chat might be interesting but will probably get you nowhere. Your information objectives should give you a pointer as to which direction to steer any conversation. This is called a semi-structured interview and it can be very useful in certain areas of field research.

The more structure you create the more like a questionnaire your research becomes. Questionnaires are valuable tools of the researcher, but need a lot of work to make them worthwhile using.

The method chosen may well depend on whether you want quasi-facts such as; Have you heard of Flash Trash? How much do you spend in restaurants in a week?, or facts such as demographic information like age, gender etc., where you could profitably use a questionnaire. Opinions (Do you prefer the government to spend on defence rather than health?) and attitudes (Would you be happier with a product which could supply these benefits?) might be better approached using semi-structured approach.

Certainly, the semi-structured approach is good for when you want a qualitative response rather than numbers as an answer. However, sooner or later you will have to put some figures together if you are to have any view on whether your plans are worth pursuing, and that is where questionnaires come into their own.

Questionnaires

You want the results of any survey to be reliable. It probably sounds axiomatic that the better the questionnaire, the more reliable the result. But it is easy to bias the results of a survey through the use of a poorly designed questionnaire. In addition, the results are expressed in numbers; 'fifty-six per cent of all passers-by said that they would shop here if I were to open'. This gives you the impression that it is reliable – it gives what I call a 'patina of verisimilitude'. So you need good questionnaire design. How do you ensure it?

There are a number of steps you have to take when putting a questionnaire before your public. Start with your objectives for the business idea. These will determine what information you need; Will it provide you with a sufficiently big income? Will it make you more attractive to the opposite sex? Will it provide you with sufficient leisure time? etc.

From these general areas will develop specific questions. For example, you are planning to discover whether if the plan will produce a good enough income – you will need to address questions such as;

- What price will I get?
- How much might I sell?
- How much will each item cost to buy, or make?
- What overheads will I insur in providing the product or service?

The last two questions are more likely answered through observation (of other similar outlets or suppliers etc.)

The first two questions led Maria Kalace to stand in the rain, talking to lorry drivers, to see if they would use her prospective Truck-Stop service, asking questions such as:

How many times per week do you have to stop out overnight:

Not at all?	[]
One night?	[]
Two nights?	[]
Three nights?	[]
over three nights?	[]

Which do you use most frequently:

Bed and breakfast?	[]
The cab?	[]
Other?	[]

How much do you normally pay each night:

Over £10?	[]
Between £5–£10?	[]
Below £5	[]

Your objectives determine your information requirements and these in turn determine the questions you need to ask.

The next step is not the design of the questionnaire but the consideration of how you will ask the questions of your target group. This will have a bearing on how you design the questionnaire.

You can get your questions in front of your prospective customers in one or a combination of three ways; face to face (a personal interview), by 'phone, or by mail.

In the first two categories the interviewer normally fills in the form and its appearance and ease of completion is less important than if you mail out the questions.

A summary of these methods leads to the following table, (*Fig. 1*).

Again you have to make a choice between the three based on your own particular set of circumstances, sometimes sacrificing reliability in favour of other factors.

	Face to Face	Telephone	Mail
Response Rate	High	Medium	Very Low
Cost/Interview – Time – Money	High High	Lowish Low/Medium	Very Low Low
Reliability	High	Medium	Medium

Fig. 1
Comparison of Methods of Delivery of Questionnaires.

The third step is to design the questionnaire to meet your needs. Design your questions to be unambiguous and preferably do not allow the respondent too much freedom in answering. Have a cut out question at the beginning:

> When Chantal Coady was investigating whether to set up Rococo, a chocolate shop in the King's Road, Chelsea she put a questionnaire to the passers by in that street. Her first question was, 'Do you ever buy chocolates?'
>
> When people responded that they did not, Chantal forgot the rest of the questionnaire, saving herself much time. (She did not forget to record the number of no answers – a very relevant piece of information for her).

You need to 'pilot' your questionnaire. This will involve testing it out with say ten or twenty people and using the subsequent insight gained to improve the questionnaire itself.

Use the pilot to discover whether the main questionnaire will answer the questions that need answers and whether you will be able to make decisions on the results.

Keep the number of questions to a minimum. Self deception is very easy here. Go back to Maria's example. How many questions are there in that extract from her questionnaire? Three you say? Actually there are eleven!

It is far better to use more than one questionnaire than trying to spend half an hour with each respondent.

Conclusion

Many people believe that the hardest part of starting a business is in deciding what you want to do at all. Having made the decision your mind automatically turns to viewing your world with a more commercial attitude and this, in turn, throws up potential business ideas by their hundreds.

I hope that this book has helped in making you decide to start generating ideas, and that it proves useful in helping you to achieve what you want from life.

Appendix I

This appendix contains some of the more important sources of information for anyone doing desk research. It has been taken from *The Small Business Guide*, Revised Edition, by C. G. T. Barrow, published by BBC Publications Ltd.

Market Research Information Sources

The A–Z of UK Marketing Data, published by Euromonitor Publications Ltd. This provides basic market data for several hundred UK markets. It ranges from adhesives to zip fasteners, and is organized by product area, market size, production, imports, exports, the main brands, their market share and a market forecast. A good glimpse at a wide range of markets.

Annual Abstract of Statistics, published by the Central Statistics Office, is the basic source of all UK statistics. Figures are given for each of the preceding ten years, so trends can be recognized.

ASLIB Directory, Volume I. Information sources in science, technology and commerce, edited by Ellen M. Coldlin, 5th edition, 1982. A valuable reference tool if you need to track down information over a wide range of subjects. This edition has over 3,000 entries from a large number of sources, professional, amateur, big and small. A major factor in including sources was their willingness to make the information available.

BBC Data Enquiry Service, Room 3, The Langham, The British Broadcasting Corporation, Portland Place, London W1A 1AA. This is a personal information service drawing on the world-wide resources of the BBC. It is an inexpensive and speedy way of checking facts and drawing on a statistical data bank which covers people, products, countries and events. The service could tell you the price of a pint of milk in 1951 or the current state of the Dutch economy. *Ad hoc* enquiries can cost as little as £5 or an annual subscription £100.

Benn's Press Directory, published by Benn Publications Ltd. Published in two volumes. Volume I is the standard reference work on the UK media, giving detailed descriptions. Volume II covers the Media in other countries.

British Business, published weekly by the Department of Industry and Trade provides basic statistics on UK markets. These include retail sales, cinemas, hire purchase, engineering sales and orders, industries' production, catering, motor trade, textiles and man-made fibre turn-overs.

British Planning Data Book, by Taylor and Redwood, published Pergamon Press Ltd, 1983. Wide ranging sources of information on Market and Industry topics.

British Rate and Data Advertisers & Agency List, Maclean-Hunter Ltd, 76 Oxford St, is produced four times a year, and lists all advertising agencies, their executives and their customers' brand names. It also covers market research and direct mail companies.

British Rate and Data, Maclean-Hunter Ltd, 76 Oxford St. updated monthly. Whatever market you are interested in, it is almost certain to have a specialised paper or journal which will be an important source of market data. *BRAD* lists all newspapers and periodicals in the UK and Eire and gives their frequency and circulation volume, price, their executives, advertising rates and readership classification.

Business Monitors, HMSO, are the medium through which the government publishes statistics it collects from over 20,000 UK firms. They are the primary and very often the only source of detailed information on the sectors they cover. *Monitors* will be able to help businessmen monitor trends and trace the progress of 4,000 individual products, manufactured by firms in 160 industries. *Monitors* can also be used to rate your business performance against that of competitors in your industry and measure the efficiency of different parts of your business.

The *Monitors* are published in three main series. The *Production Monitors* are published monthly, quarterly and annually. The quarterly is probably the most useful, with comprehensive yet timely, information. The *Service and Distribution Monitors* cover the retail market, the instalment credit business, the motor trade, catering and allied trades and the computer service industry, among others. Finally there are *Miscellaneous Monitors* covering such topics as shipping, insurance, import/export ratios for industry, acquisitions and mergers of industrial and commercial companies, cinemas and tourism.

The Annual Census of Production Monitors cover virtually every sector of industry, and include data on total purchases, total sales, stocks, work in progress, capital expenditure, employment, wages and salaries. They include analyses of costs and output, of establishments by size, of full and part-time employees by sex, and of employment, net capital expenditure and net output by region.

You can use the information – particularly that from the size analysis table – to establish such ratios as gross output per head, net to gross output, and wages and salaries to net output. With these as a base, you can compare the performance of your own business with the average for firms of similar size, and for that with your particular industry as a whole. For example, you can discover your share of the market, and compare employment figures, increases in sales and so on.

Many central libraries will have a selection of the *Business Monitor* series. Individual monitors can be bought from HMSO Books, PO Box 569, London SE1 9NH.

Financial Times Business Information Service, published by the Financial Times.

Guide to Official Statistics, published by HMSO, is the main guide to all government produced statistics, including *ad hoc* reports. However, a brief, free guide is available from the Press and Information Service, Central Statistical Office, Great George Street, London SW1 3AQ.

Index to Business Reports, edited by R. N. Hunter, published by Headland Press. This provides the key to thousands of market and industrial reports. Latest volumes published Jan. 1983–Dec. 1984.

Key Note Publications. Published by Key Note Publications. They produce concise briefs on various sectors of the UK economy. Each *Key Note* contains a detailed examination of the structure of an industry, its distribution network and its major companies; an in-depth analysis of the market, covering products by volume and value, market shares, foreign trade and an appraisal of trends within the market; a review of recent developments in the industry, highlighting new product development, corporate development and legislation; a financial analysis of named major companies, providing data and ratios over a three-year period together with a corporate appraisal and economic overview; forecasts on the future prospects for the industry, including estimates from *Key Note's* own database and authoritative trade sources. There is a very useful appendix detailing further sources of information – recent press articles, other reports and journals.

Over 100 market sectors are covered, including such areas as adhesives, after-dinner drinks, bicycles, butchers, commercial leasing, health foods, road haulage, public houses, travel agents and women's magazines.

Marketing and distribution abstracts, published eight times a year by Anbar Publications Ltd. This surveys 200 journals world-wide and provides an index to abstracts of appropriate articles in the field.

Index

Compiled by Michael J. Heary